How to Increase Employee Competence

How to Increase Employee Competence

Norman C. Hill

Exxon Company
New Orleans, Louisiana

McGraw-Hill Book Company

New York   St. Louis   San Francisco   Auckland   Bogotá   Hamburg
Johannesburg   London   Madrid   Mexico   Montreal   New Delhi
Panama   Paris   São Paulo   Singapore   Sydney   Tokyo   Toronto

Library of Congress Cataloging in Publication Data

Hill, Norman C.
    How to increase employee competence.

    Includes index.
    1. Personnel management.   2. Organizational behavior.
I. Title
HF5549.H477   1984   658.3'14   83-25603
ISBN 0-07-028790-2

1234567890   DOC/DOC   8987654

ISBN 0-07-028790-2

The editors for this book were Martha Jewett and Joan Cipriano, the designer was Al Cetta, and the production supervisor was Thomas G. Kowalczyk. It was set in Zapf Book Light by Bi-Comp, Incorporated.
Printed and bound by R. R. Donnelley & Sons Company.

Contents

Chapter 3:   Beliefs, Symbols, and Words   31

Part II: Interpersonal Processes   41

Chapter 4:   Self-Esteem and the Self-Fulfilling Prophecy in Management   43

Chapter 5:   Counseling Employees: Developing Problem-Solving Skills and Enhancing Competence   58

Chapter 6: Career Assessment and Development 85

Chapter 7: The Uses of Recognition and Feedback 103

Part III: Organizational Processes 115

Chapter 8: Team Building: Potential, Pitfalls, and Prospects 117

Chapter 9: Clarifying and Establishing Expectations: A Management Function 127

Preface

If we define situations as real, they are real in their consequences.
—W. I. Thomas

There are many current books and articles which extol the virtues of "pulling your own strings" and "looking out for number one." Such self-help topics are neither new nor recent. Maxwell Maltz, Norman Vincent Peale, Clement Stone, and others who wrote a generation ago were just as cogent as more modern authors in describing the virtues of taking charge of life and becoming successful. It is an ingrained American impulse, moreover, that anyone can succeed through hard work and determined effort. We are, after all, Horatio Alger's children.

Since we believe in such possibilities, we structure our world to obtain our goals. We look for ways to become what we want to be and follow the advice of those who have apparently "made it." And there are many who are willing to tell us their secrets of how to look, act, and speak the parts. "Success!" according to writer Michael Korda depends more on looking the part than knowing it. The biggest fools in the world, Korda says, are the people who merely do their work supremely well without attending to appearances.

Appearances in Korda's world are nearly everything. He shows how to sit at meetings, how to wear a suit coat, and how to use glasses to emphasize a point. Such a dependence on what others think, however, carries significant liabilities. As suggested by the protagonist in the novel *Portnoy's Complaint*, this dependence forces people to operate within a thin zone of acceptance. Instead of accepting mistakes and social guffaws as a normal part of experience, this type of thinking makes us intolerant of any mistakes made by others and paranoid about our own. Thus, we become paralyzed by inaction for fear that we will be doing something wrong.

Although we would like to think Korda's world is a myth, it isn't. For instance, an acquaintance of mine who is a managing partner for a Big Eight accounting firm recently returned from a planning meeting with other senior managers and reported to junior members in his firm on some of the selection criteria for advancement. After describing the value of initiative and hard work, he indicated that some potential candidates were not well regarded because they were overweight and preferred corduroy suits. The manager was sincere and well-intentioned in wanting to discuss factors which junior members should know about and incorporate into their work habits. He did not realize that he was emphasizing appearance over substance.

Such an emphasis on appearance has a very debilitating effect on people. It makes us self-conscious. It suggests that no one can be trusted and that personal values and independence matter very little. It is the caricature described in William H. Whyte's *Organization Man*—a chameleon who changes with the environment.

Although people may attain some degree of success by following this, they will not be very effective in their work relationships. Effectiveness is based on competence. Effective, competent employees have very clear values and a determined sense of personal security. They have a strong sense of who they are, and this, like a gyroscope, provides stability and direction in their lives. It is not that they are unaffected by others, but rather that they seek out people with similar values and work orientations who reinforce one another.

We do not exist in a vacuum. We are affected by others and by circumstances. We are, to a very large degree, what we think important others in our lives think we are. That is a human process. Despite our best efforts, we care what other people think and are affected by their approval or disapproval. Although we cannot eliminate such processes—like gravity, they simply exist without necessarily being good or bad—we can use them to our advantage if we understand how they work. We can increase our competence—the ability to get things done—and the competence of others if we have the know-how and are willing to utilize it.

This book is a reflection of my own search for understanding about how people in organizations get things done. It is a product of my own observation and research and does not necessarily represent the opinion of Exxon or any of its managers. It am appreciative of the many "important others" who have assisted and encouraged me in this project. J. B. Ritchie and I first wrote a very academic and theoretical article in 1977 from which my study on the process of self-esteem has been largely derived. Gene W. Dalton has continually encouraged me to bridge the worlds of those who manage large organizations and those who typically study them. They are both good friends and mentors. Joan Lopez has typed and retyped this manuscript and provided suggestions and assistance in its preparation. My family members deserve more than mere acknowledgment for their support and patience while I was completing this manuscript. E. E. Cummings once noted that "unless you love someone, nothing else matters." I am grateful for my immediate and my extended families with whom I am able to share my life and to whom I have given my loyalty.

Part I

Individual Processes

Chapter 1

A Time for Change

It has been a long day for Gary, and he's glad it's almost over. He's been working a lot of overtime in order to complete a special project for his boss. Even though he's a day late, he'll be able to provide a lot of extra backup material in his report by taking the additional time. As he finishes proofreading the final pages, his boss sticks his head in the door and brusquely says, "I've got a plane to catch. Are you finished with your report so that I can read it on the way?" As Gary gives it to him, his boss sarcastically mutters an almost inaudible "thanks" then is gone. Afterward, Gary wonders, "Was he upset with me because I didn't finish on time? I bet he sees me as unable to ever meet deadlines and will never give me anything that has a firm deadline again. He probably thinks I'm lazy and uncommitted. Did I screw up that time!"

Sound familiar? Even if the situation doesn't precisely describe something that has happened to you, most of us can at least recognize the sentiments being expressed as ones we have felt from time to time. We try hard. We want to do our best. We work furiously to finish something, only to have it seemingly curtly accepted. And we say to ourselves, "I messed up. I did it again. Somebody else, anybody else could have done it better."

We blame ourselves for not measuring up, all on the basis of a reply—verbal or nonverbal—from our supervisor.

Take another situation. The noon hour is nearly over as Janice rushes through the cafeteria line. She spies some coworkers from another office that she is acquainted with but doesn't know very well. As she smiles and asks to sit down, someone at the table says, "Sure," but adds, "We were just leaving. Catch you later, okay?" Instead of shrugging off the incident, Janice wonders, "Did they really have to go, or did they not want to eat with me? It seems like they don't want anything to do with me. What's wrong? What's wrong with me?"

At various times, nearly all of us experience situations like this: we try our best, but it seems that our best isn't good enough. Then, we wonder, "What's wrong with me that I keep getting brushed off or brushed aside?" We question our competence, our ability, even our desirability. Maybe they're right, we say to ourselves. Maybe, they're right, Gary says to himself. Maybe I don't work very well when I have a deadline to meet and should ask for a transfer to a different kind of job. Maybe they're right, Janice says to herself. Maybe I'm not very interesting. They don't like me because I'm a social incompetent.

This process of explaining things to ourselves is a continuous one. Events occur, things happen, situations develop, and we create explanations about why they occurred, developed, or happened the way that they did. We attribute reasons to what happens to us to help explain our part in the events that transpire day to day in either our personal or our professional lives. We like things to be predictable and explainable, and that is why we attribute reasons to events even when our information is incomplete.

Gary and Janice, like most people, usually shrug off the cold shoulder or the apparent slight. The boss is in a hurry, Gary may say at another time to himself. I am late in going to lunch today, Janice might mutter aloud on another occasion. But when we are under stress, or putting forth our best efforts, or trying very hard, we may not react in so calm and logical a manner. We tell ourselves not to take it personally, but we do anyway. We were surprised by an unexpected response, an unexpected reaction, and so we are less likely to explain such incidences to ourselves in a manner that does not include some personal blame.

We often explain our failures by telling ourselves "I am incompetent" instead of "I didn't try hard enough." Or we interpret a social rebuff as "I am undesirable" instead of "That person is preoccupied with something else." We give ourselves reasons for why things occur that include self-blame that is final and irrevocable. There is a huge difference between "I am a failure" and "I have failed." One seems unchangeable, a birthmark, the other a description of events.

Some of us, when we feel uncertain or insecure or under stress, talk with others about the conclusions we may reach following some type of incident to see if they would interpret it the same way. This process enables us to do "reality testing" to determine if we are reading too much into a situation, making more of it than was there. This interaction is healthy because it also allows us to get whatever may be a concern out in the open, thus giving us the opportunity "to blow off steam." But others of us—bruised by the brusque remark, frazzled by another's frown— keep our hurts to ourselves. We talk to no one because we are afraid or embarrassed, or think no one else understands. We want to hide our hurt and, so, like a cat look for a corner to slink off to and rest.

If we let such negative feelings and self-defeating beliefs about our- selves pile up, it may be difficult for us to see our achievements in their true light. We discount the praise of others by saying it was nothing or tell ourselves that others would have done it better had they been given the chance. A social gaffe, a misunderstanding with the boss, a run-in with a coworker may all add up to personal conclusions we might reach sug- gesting that "I'm not good with people. I should get a different job." A job rejection or work that is turned back to be redone may produce an "I'm past my prime" or "I'm just a loser." When we experience several failures, we may conclude we're incompetent, period. No room for change.

Sometimes when we fail, it's simply because of our misdirected efforts or lack of effort in the first place. We simply didn't pay the price for success. We err, however, when we blame ourselves and conclude that we are incapable of ever doing well. If we've been waiting for a promotion and are passed over, or we've been hoping for a particular assignment and it goes to someone else, it may be difficult for us to examine the reasons logically without jumping to self-incriminating conclusions. At the same time, we shouldn't completely switch gears and secretly blame others or office politics for such disappointments—that can lead to feel- ings of resignation and hopelessness and prevent us from changing things that may need changing.

Self-Esteem—A Perspective

Popular books and articles on increasing self-esteem abound. Such ad- vice ranges from *Dressing for Success* to *Think and Grow Rich*—titles from two well-known books. Although it is apparent that procedures outlined in such material have some effect, the results have been largely overstated. Moreover, although dress and individuality certainly reflect a self-confident person, they are not the keys to that person's develop- ment.

Erik Erikson, a prominent psychologist who has intensely studied the process of adult development, suggests that one gains confidence only by moving from one crisis to another. In his "catastrophe theory" of development he maintains that we are continually confronted with life tasks that test us and try us. These crises are predictable and proceed along an expected continuum. Erikson suggests that self-mastery is achieved when one moves successfully from the crisis that he terms "identity vs. role diffusion"—that is, the finding of one's role in society, so that society sends back a confirming role about who one is—to the crisis of "intimacy vs. isolation"—the desire to be committed strongly to someone or something—and finally moves to "generativity"—helping and guiding others. Unfulfilled expectations or incomplete resolutions at one stage make it difficult to move on to the next stage. This source of ambivalence produces anxiety which may affect one's confidence: most of us don't recognize a crisis until it has passed. While we are in the midst of moving from one stage to another, it may seem that all is chaos and confusion.

Most of us, however, don't develop in so linear a manner. Our progress is seldom a continuous straight line of moving onward and upward. It is instead more often characterized by sudden discontinuities, surprises, and twists. We have preoccupations, false starts, and diversions that make development difficult and make mere survival seem a minor triumph.

Understanding How People Work

Any individual can be thought of as a diverse set of social selves organized around a basic self-image or self-concept. If the person feels good about who he or she is, self-esteem is said to be high. If the person has a low opinion of self, low aspirations, or a self-conception that suggests he or she is unimportant, self-esteem is low. Everyone has a basic temperament, an intelligence factor, and psychological defenses that are chronic and enduring. But people also have learned ways of coping with situational pressures that basically determine their self-image and the kinds of social selves the person will construct to deal with his or her environment.

Self-esteem is an evaluation we make about ourselves that is continually changing. It is based on our beliefs about our competence in each of the roles we adopt: parent, spouse, friend, citizen, employee, etc. How we determine our role in each of the situations we face, and how capably we think we fulfill the role requirements, powerfully influence our behavior. Better understanding our roles, their requirements, and our behavior in them can help us be more effective in achieving the outcomes that we desire. This concept of constructed social selves is one that has been employed by a variety of theorists and researchers. This theory suggests that the way people think, feel, and behave is a product of how they have interacted with others in the past and what they perceive to be expected of them in various roles in the present. This perspective does not deny the existence of basic personality traits, but it maintains that personality traits tell little about how a person acts or reacts in various situations. For example, someone may have a personality structure that revolves around the repression of strong aggressive impulses, may be temperamentally easily frustrated, and may rely upon denial as a common defense mechanism whenever backed into a corner. These characteristics may describe the person's basic personality, but they say little about that person's self-image, how he or she behaves in occupational or social roles, how he or she interacts with others, and the like.

Focusing on someone's constructed self, on the other hand, shows how he or she interacts with others and the impact this interaction has on how that person thinks, feels, and behaves. People with the same kind of personality structure might enter into similar interactive situations quite differently. In other words if a manager or someone else is interested in improving someone's motivation to work, the manager should take note of the person's constructed self in various interaction situations as a key place to begin in working with that person. A major implication of this approach is that an employee cannot remain lazy and unmotivated, have poor work habits, and be unwilling to take initiative without the interactional support of others. People are unmotivated only to the extent that their interaction patterns with others reinforce this perspective. To change someone, a manager must alter that person's view of himself or herself—a view that is only constant to the extent that interaction patterns remain unchanged.

All our past interaction patterns become a part of us. We catalog them and call upon them in new situations if we think that they will work for us—give us the predictability and control we desire. To a large extent, we are not conscious of the almost instantaneous choices we make among possible options as we compose ourselves when we encounter a new situation. The changes which occur in us during the course of our careers are changes in the nature of these constructed selves. It is highly unlikely that we will substantively change our basic personality structure, but we can and do drastically change our constructed selves in that we develop new attitudes and values, adopt new images of ourselves, acquire new competencies, and create new ways of thinking, feeling, and behaving. This process of developing people is one that every manager and every human resource professional should be familiar with in order to tap the potential of employees at work.

Self-Esteem and Productive Functioning

Research from a variety of sources verifies that increasing the self-esteem of people is the key to their improved performance. Consider the following:

- The work of Richard Hackman (Yale) has illustrated the fact that people will not take advantage of enriched jobs if they do not possess a certain high level of self-esteem. The key to improved motivation, Hackman has found, lies both in job characteristics and in individual self-esteem.[1]

- Paul Lawrence's (Harvard) research on conditions that affect job satisfaction maintains that a high correlation exists between such job satisfaction and individual self-esteem.[2]

- George Strauss (California–Berkeley) completed an extensive review on the tools and technology of organization development (OD) and concluded that what made OD work were changes in the self-esteem of participants.[3] Unsuccessful OD efforts could be identified by the lack of attention paid to this factor.

- Abraham Korman (Michigan) has provided a lot of evidence to support a theory of motivation that centers on one's beliefs about one's self.[4] Korman maintains that (1) people attempt to behave in a manner consistent with their own self-image; (2) if employees see themselves as failures on the job, they will not put forth much effort, their performance will be poor, and a self-reinforcing cycle will be set in motion; and consequently (3) the most successful managerial strategy to improve performance will focus on enhancing employees' self-images.

- The successful work of David McClelland[5] (Harvard) and of most management by objectives (MBO) strategies is aimed at altering individual aspiration levels. If management establishes high performance expectations, employees will work out the details of getting there. All they need is a target to shoot for that stretches them.

- Gene Dalton's (Brigham Young University) comprehensive review on how people and organizations change emphasizes that successful efforts are predicated on an increase in self-esteem.[6] Without this foreseeable outcome, people will be unlikely to support any new ways of doing things.

It could be argued that any attempt to enhance the competency of one's self or others is an attempt to improve self-esteem. Unfortunately, many instructional programs fail because they do not provide activities or events that make this possible. There is an old French saying that maintains that "to teach French to Tommy, one must know not only French, but also Tommy." It isn't enough for an instructor to be familiar with a particular subject matter; he or she must be knowledgeable about the students. Likewise, a manager who is interested in performance improvement through counseling must know and understand each employee as well as the counseling process itself.

Years ago management training programs in industry stressed the importance of managerial self-insight. Awareness was viewed as the key to managerial performance. How managers reacted to power, conflict, dependency, and other issues was the focus of seminars and schools. But this approach seemed less practical and pragmatic than was needed for the busy manager. Something more hard-hitting and "everydayish" appeared to be more appropriate, so training programs began emphasizing this approach of enumerating pragmatic techniques for managing.

Although every training program must be based on predetermined needs identified at the time, training seminars ought to take note of both pragmatism and self-awareness. Importantly, timing and sequencing can make all the difference in the world. Self-insight sets the stage for building skills. One must become aware of inadequacies or opportunities before being interested in developing skills for doing things differently.

Those who manage organizations and are interested in improving the performance of people they supervise must know how to develop their own self-esteem as well as that of others. If we understand the kind of person we are in general, our roots, and where we are headed, we will present ourselves as capable and competent in interaction situations. Others will pick up on this self-confidence as well, and it will become self-reinforcing. Self-esteem is neither arrogance nor ignorance. It is an evaluation which we all make and customarily maintain of ourselves. It expresses our belief at the moment in our capabilities.

By reflecting on the causes, correlates, and consequences of self-esteem, we gain important benefits. First, by explicitly analyzing the nature and dimensions of individual self-esteem, we begin to objectify it and see it for what it really is. We see self-esteem as a developmental process that can be enhanced or degraded. We see it as something that can be influenced. Knowing that, we can begin to lay the groundwork for a rational plan of intervention and change.

The Self-Esteem Process

How people regard themselves is a product of a very distinct process. Recognizing the various aspects of this process provides "intervention

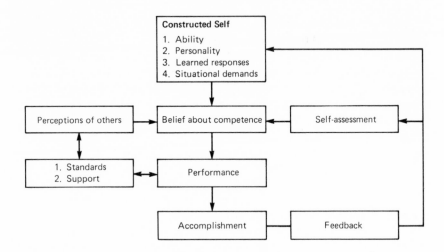

points" for taking action. The model shown in the above illustration represents the basic process by which people develop their own self-image and shows ways self-regard can be enhanced. From this overview, it is clear that individually we exert some control on how we will perform, but we are also influenced by the perceptions of others.

Evaluating Yourself: Where to Start

The way we think about ourselves has profound effects on every aspect of our lives. What we think we can do will significantly affect what activities we will attempt and our evaluation of our efforts. Most people restrict their own potentialities. We are taught throughout our lives certain attitudes that limit our growth and effectiveness. For instance, many of us are taught that we should understand our weakness as well as we can so that we can plan the appropriate steps to improve our proficiency. Sometimes we become so preoccupied with wanting to overcome our deficiencies that we fail to recognize what we are good at and build upon our strengths.

Our own self-evaluations can sometimes be overly critical to the extent that we do not give ourselves a chance to succeed. We falter before we even try. We make impossible comparisons and back away from tasks we think we will not be able to perform adequately. Self-esteem is an evaluation of our own worth based on our own perceptions of how we compare with others and how we perceive that significant others in our lives view us. We all do it. We all make these comparisons and evaluations and think about how we're measuring up. Sometimes we try to ignore the opinions of others and say to ourselves, "What do they know? So what if he thinks I'm a slouch; I know I'm not." We may even remember the children's rhyme "Sticks and stones may break my bones, but names will never hurt me," but it has a hollow ring to it. Other people matter. We want to be respected, admired, thought highly of by *certain* people in *certain* areas. But impossible comparisons or trying too hard to please others can result in timidity and apprehension, a feeling that we will never be fully accepted for who we are but must continually prove ourselves.

SELF-ESTEEM ASSESSMENT QUESTIONNAIRE

Instructions: *Circle the number which most accurately describes your thoughts, feelings, and actions. Notice that the evaluation categories vary from Part A to Part B and again in Part C. Add your responses and record your subtotal scores at the end of each section.*

Section I: Individual Process

Part A

	Rarely	Sometimes	About half of the time	More often than not	Nearly always
• I believe that almost anyone could do my job just as well as I. There's nothing that unique about my contribution.	5	4	3	2	1
• I believe that I am not meeting my life's ambitions because of factors outside of my control.	5	4	3	2	1
• I am fearful about making mistakes and get the feeling that one wrong move will mean the loss of prestige I have gained in my work so far in my career.	5	4	3	2	1
• The best part of my job is that I know how to do it. I would be concerned about doing a job with more responsibility because I would not want to try something and fail at it.	5	4	3	2	1
• When I compare who I am with who I hoped to be at this stage in my life and/or career, I feel discouraged.	5	4	3	2	1

Part B	Rarely	Sometimes	About half of the time	More often than not	Nearly always
• I believe that if I really try and have the right training, there isn't anything I can't do.	1	2	3	4	5
• I don't think luck or fate is very real. People who work hard get what they want; others who don't, complain.	1	2	3	4	5
• I know how to do what is expected of me.	1	2	3	4	5
• There are several things I can point to as being special skills or unique abilities.	1	2	3	4	5
• I think I have a good sense of who I am and what my life is about. I can be realistic about my limits and my capabilities.	1	2	3	4	5

Part C	Yesterday	Last week	Last month	Some months ago	Can't remember when
• The last time I tried something new that required different skills or involved activities that were unfamiliar to me was _____.	5	4	3	2	1
• The last time I made a written list of personal goals was _____.	5	4	3	2	1
• The last time I can honestly say I did something for someone else which no one knew about was _____.	5	4	3	2	1
• The last time I accomplished a personal goal or objective was _____.	5	4	3	2	1
• The most recent event or activity that I can point to with pride as an accomplishment occurred _____.	5	4	3	2	1
Subtotal I					

Section II: Perceptions of Others

Part A

	Rarely	Sometimes	About half of the time	More often than not	Nearly always
• If my boss were to call me into his or her office unexpectedly and close the door, my first thought would be "Oh, no, what have I done now?"	5	4	3	2	1
• The people I work with think I'm okay, but I don't think any of them are really my friends.	5	4	3	2	1
• I often feel compelled to be successful because I have been in the past and now others expect it of me.	5	4	3	2	1
• There often seems to be a lack of trust between me and the people with whom I work.	5	4	3	2	1
• I'm not really sure what other people at work think about me—and frankly, I don't care how I'm viewed.	5	4	3	2	1

Part B

	Rarely	Sometimes	About half of the time	More often than not	Nearly always
• I think that most people who know me at work also like me.	1	2	3	4	5
• I think my opinion is generally respected and I'm valued for what I contribute.	1	2	3	4	5
• I don't feel threatened by my boss or colleagues.	1	2	3	4	5
• I trust other people with personal confidences and think that I'm trusted as well.	1	2	3	4	5
• I don't have to watch my words or be overly cautious about what I say at work.	1	2	3	4	5

Part C	Yesterday	Last week	Last month	Some months ago	Can't remember when
• The last time someone confided a personal problem with me was _____ .	5	4	3	2	1
• The last time someone offered to help me with a project that I was working on was _____ .	5	4	3	2	1
• The last time a colleague gave me a sincere compliment was _____ .	5	4	3	2	1
• The last time someone asked my advice on something that was outside my area of responsibility but of which I have some knowledge was _____ .	5	4	3	2	1
• The last time I discussed my dreams, goals, or hopes with someone else was _____ .	5	4	3	2	1
Subtotal II					

Section III: Organizational Demands *Part A*	Rarely	Sometimes	About half of the time	More often than not	Nearly always
• I often feel caught between conflicting demands from my supervisor or staff or others.	5	4	3	2	1
• Higher-level managers don't really want people here to express their true opinions. People who get ahead are ones who always agree.	5	4	3	2	1
• What is expected of me is unrealistic. It is not possible to meet the expectations of this job.	5	4	3	2	1
• There is great pressure for employees to dress, behave, and think alike.	5	4	3	2	1
• I have little influence over things which affect me at work.	5	4	3	2	1

Part B	Rarely	Sometimes	About half of the time	More often than not	Nearly always
• I have a lot of influence over what happens to me at work. I feel in control of things.	1	2	3	4	5
• I can complete job assignments by working steadily. I find the pressure that I have stimulating rather than a problem.	1	2	3	4	5
• The authority that I have to do my job is adequate.	1	2	3	4	5
• I am able to keep my personal, professional, and family demands in balance without feeling overextended.	1	2	3	4	5
• The rules and policies in this organization make sense and are there for a purpose.	1	2	3	4	5

Part C	Yesterday	Last week	Last month	Some months ago	Can't remember when
• The last time that I went home from work really feeling good (whistling, humming a tune, etc.) was _____.	5	4	3	2	1
• The last time my boss recognized my work on a project was _____.	5	4	3	2	1
• The most recent time a spouse, friend, or colleague wished me a good day at work was _____.	5	4	3	2	1
• The last time I really felt in control over the work projects and priorities I have was _____.	5	4	3	2	1
• The last time my boss asked my opinion on something that was not in my direct area of responsibility was _____.	5	4	3	2	1
Subtotal III					

Section I   **Subtotal** _____

Section II   **Subtotal** _____

Section III   **Subtotal** _____

           TOTAL =============

In developing or maintaining your own self-esteem, it is useful to have as clear a perception as possible of your own ability and the conditions in your environment which support or boycott your sense of competence. We do not live in a vacuum but in a world of colliding ideals, egos, and aspirations. The preceding exercise provided a self-assessment tool for measuring your own self-esteem and the conditions in various facets of your life which influence it.

Scoring Your Responses

Since this questionnaire is intended primarily as a self-assessment device, obviously there are no right or wrong answers. In evaluating your own responses, check the consistency of your answers from Part A to Part B to Part C. If you find large discrepancies, you may wish to reevaluate your responses. The questionnaire is divided into three primary sections which correspond to three primary processes involved in developing self-esteem.

Interestingly, people who are independently evaluated by their peers as possessing high self-esteem typically score themselves as only between 50 and 60 on this instrument. Interviews with those who score beyond this range reveal individuals who are often anxious to please and so evaluate their current life experiences on the questionnaire as excessively positive. This "overdependence" on others and its debilitating effects are explored in subsequent chapters. Those with lower scores, especially in Section III—Organizational Demands—believe that they are at the mercy of vast powerful forces "out there" over which they have little influence. Although your personal scores may or may not indicate a propensity toward any of these areas, they can be useful as a beginning point in determining a personal development agenda.

Summary

Self-esteem is a conclusion I reach about myself, an assessment of my abilities, partially influenced by what important others think about me. Thus, improving how I assess and evaluate my abilities and the things which happen to me everyday will also be useful in enhancing my self-esteem. The story told about three famous baseball umpires may serve as a useful illustration. Each was asked by a sports editor how he determined the difference between balls and strikes. The first umpire said, "Some are balls and some are strikes; I call 'em the way I see 'em." The second umpire gave the same reply. The third umpire thought for a moment and then remarked, "Some are balls and some are strikes, but they ain't nothin' until I call 'em."

So it is with us and how we size up a situation. Our conclusion about our capabilities certainly has some relationship to our actual performance, but capability and performance are not the same. Improving our ability to assess our competence and evaluate our future possibilities is important in building self-esteem. Of course, these same skills are essential in assisting others in building their self-esteem as well. In this chapter and the ones which follow, research case studies and exercises are presented which explain various ways work-related competencies can be enhanced. It is important to recognize that self-esteem is *not* simply an individual characteristic even though it includes individual processes. It is, instead, situational and also incorporates interpersonal and organizational processes.

This book is essentially a manual for change. It shows how you can change yourself as well as others. It describes important processes in such change efforts: how to give counsel and advice, how to assess and develop career potentials, how to improve work group and organizational behavior. Chapters in each of these areas describe important results and how to obtain them. They are not narrowly focused. Instead they describe ways and means to develop the competency of people at work and increase the likelihood that their contributions will also be self-satisfying. Showing how individual desires and organizational demands can be meshed as effectively as possible is the goal of each chapter.

References

1. Hackman, J. Richard: "Work Design," in J. R. Hackman and J. L. Suttle (eds.), *Improving Life at Work: Behavioral Science Approaches to Organizational Change* (Santa Monica, Calif.: Goodyear, 1977).

2. Cited in Katzell, Raymond, et al.: *Work, Productivity and Job Satisfaction* (New York: Harcourt, Brace, and Jovanovich, 1975).

3. Strauss, George: *Organizational Behavior* (Belmont, Calif.: Wadsworth, 1976).

4. Korman, Abraham: *Industrial and Organizational Psychology* (Englewood Cliffs, N.J.: Prentice-Hall, 1971).

5. McClelland, David C.: "Achievement Motivation Can Be Developed," *Harvard Business Review* (March–April, 1965), pp. 6–24.

6. Dalton, Gene W.: "Influence and Organizational Change," in J. B. Ritchie and P. H. Thompson (eds.), *Organization and People* (St. Paul, Minn.: West, 1980).

Chapter 2

Increasing Your Self-Confidence

Factors which have appeared repeatedly in the findings of published reports on productive functioning are self-confidence and self-esteem. Apparently, people who are productive and effective possess a favorable attitude toward themselves and their ability to handle a variety of situations and events. This attitude has been described in various ways. The terms "ego strength," "self-respect," and "self-actualization" are more or less synonymous with the two designations which will be used interchangeably here: self-esteem and self-confidence. All these terms suggest a positive evaluation of one's self, of one's competence and ability, and of one's personal judgment of worthiness.

Self-esteem and self-confidence are highly dependent on the degree to which people's successes approach their expectations in those areas which are important to them. Too high expectations or too few successes can jeopardize people's positive views of themselves. So too can negative evaluations by significant others in a person's world. Although self-esteem reflects the self-evaluation people make of themselves, this evaluation is in turn heavily dependent on the evaluation that they believe important others are making of them.

"I'm not in competition with David Rockefeller," one middle manager has said. "I only want to do well in terms of me." It seems apparent that the closer we get to the standards (whatever they are) which we have in our heads, the better we are going to feel about ourselves and the things we do. And the better we feel, the better we do.

Research Evidence

Several studies have demonstrated that self-esteem or self-confidence is indeed a significant factor in managerial effectiveness. In 1948, B. B. Gardner wrote a book entitled *What Makes Successful and Unsuccessful Executives?*[1] He answered his question by saying that those who possessed a clear sense of identity and knew what they wanted and how to achieve it were promoted sooner and more often than their colleagues who believed that they were not as admirable or as worthy as they should be.

Another investigation which established a relationship between self-esteem and personal success is a study begun in 1922.[2] Approximately 1400 adolescents between the ages of 10 and 11 with genius-level IQs, a status which placed them in the top 1 percent of the nation's population, were identified by researchers. In follow-up surveys in 1940 and 1950 (when participants were in their early thirties and forties), three factors were found which distinguished the most successful from the least successful. These were integration toward goals, perseverance, and self-confidence. Apparently, those who were the most successful recognized both their abilities and their limitations, were reasonable in their aspirations and expectations, and were undaunted in pursuing them.

Some research done by David Moment and Abraham Zaleznick at the Harvard Business School also justifies singling out self-confidence as a way to managerial effectiveness.[3] Moment and Zaleznick studied people in middle and upper management and had coworkers rate these managers' abilities to present ideas, guide a discussion, provide leadership, and develop friendships. Those who were rated high on each dimension were designated "stars," those who were high in all but the congenial categories were called "technical specialists," those high only in the congenial categories were labeled "social specialists," and the rest were classified as "underchosen."

The researchers tested each group extensively and reported that the stars were different from the other three groups in one significant way: the confidence they had in themselves. The stars thought of themselves as efficient and competent, able to meet any challenge given to them. They felt they could defend a position while remaining flexible in their outlook and were devoid of the Machiavellian arrogance that is often thought to accompany a high degree of self-confidence. Those in the technical specialist group were noted for their good ideas, but tended to be evasive in expressing their feelings about other people and consequently were less effective in dealing with committees, groups, and individuals. The social specialists, although involved with others, displayed rather dependent behavior. They appeared to need a lot of support from other people and to value friendships more then productivity. The underchosen had markedly low self-esteem and were reported as characteristically defensive, bitter, cynical, critical, and uncooperative.

Few people will openly say they feel inadequate or worthless in a managerial situation. They may, however, express those feelings indirectly in the degree of pessimism or optimism with which they go about their work. People with a positive sense of self-worth, on the other hand, typically display poise and radiate their inner confidence. They are the participators, the initiators, the leaders in an organization who keep the entire social machinery moving and producing. It is easy for them to be optimists—they usually get what they go after.

The stars, in the Moment and Zaleznick study, were stars because they believed in themselves. Coworkers believed in them too, and that belief served to reinforce the stars' view of what they thought they could do. In contrast, the underchosen didn't like themselves very well. They tended to be suspicious of other people, believing that others were trying to get them, to use them in some way, or to work some kind of angle. People with low self-esteem do not like themselves very well, and other people tend to regard them similarly. After all, if someone doesn't think much of himself or herself, why should others.

In another research project done at the Harvard Business School, self-esteem was again determined to significantly distinguish more productive managers from their less productive counterparts.[4] Abraham Zaleznick, Gene Dalton, and Louis Barnes categorized the managers and professionals of a large firm as "oriented" or "conflicted" regarding their performance aspirations and personal plans. Those who were labeled "oriented" possessed attitudes and values consistent with their aspirations while the "conflicted" group were those whose aspirations were inconsistent with their values.

Those in the oriented group were rated as more effective managers by colleagues than those in the conflicted group. Apparently the factor which distinguished the oriented and conflicted managers was not training or ability, but self-esteem. The oriented managers tended to exhibit a great deal of confidence in their own abilities, had a basic trust in their work relationships, and possessed an excellent ability to concentrate on intellectual endeavors. The conflicted managers, however, were not less intelligent or less capable, but they were less self-assured. They demanded either sympathy or reward for their efforts and tended to take criticism personally.

People who see themselves as competent and capable do not crumble with criticism. Rather, they view it as a natural outgrowth of the essential task of assessing and evaluating performance. However, people with low self-esteem tend to view any critique as negative criticism and see it as simply confirming their inadequacy. They generally discount compliments and praise as well. Such figures of speech as "It was no big deal" and "You're just saying that to make me feel good," either uttered or unexpressed, represent ways in which such people discount the praise they receive.

Managers who feel confident in most social interactions and who have a high sense of personal worth are successful because they are able to act quickly and decisively in pressure situations. Since management is characterized by an almost innumerable number of activities that require quick action and ad hoc wisdom, people who are not plagued by self-doubt or disillusionment are naturally going to fit in better with the demands of the job. To be able to work effectively in spite of frequent interruptions, to coordinate and direct the activities of others, to perform at an unrelenting pace—all characteristics of managerial work—require the type of people who believe in themselves and their own abilities.

Dynamic Self-Esteem

All of us see ourselves in some way—bright, beautiful, eager, shrewd, misunderstood, steady, aggressive, dull, shy, or some other kind of adjective. We can all pick out one or two phrases that we believe describe ourselves if we are given a wide enough range of choices. We all see ourselves in some very distinct ways, some good and some no so good. This image of ourselves is important because everything we do or say, everything we think, hear, feel, or believe is influenced by how we see ourselves.

It is apparent that this internal view of ourselves is learned. It is not inherited and it is not static. Rather, it is a product of all that has happened to us from the moment of life and of how we have come to regard these events. As our experiences multiply, new events must somehow fit into the categories we have created for ourselves. If the experiences we have as we grow older do not fit into existing boxes, then the experiences or the boxes or both must be modified. Most of the time, the categories stay and the events are filtered into them. In this way, we create our own reality.

This view of ourselves tells us how we should approach each new experience or event as well. If our view of ourselves suggests that each new experience contains something to be learned—has some potential for filling up an empty category—then we are likely to approach new tasks with confidence. If, on the other hand, our view of ourselves suggests that new experiences are stressful and will turn out bad—not fit into existing categories—we will probably approach new tasks with apprehension. People develop not by adjusting themselves to their physical environment but by transforming their environment either through productive work or through their filters of reality.

No one escapes disappointments or negative experiences in life. However, the person who is able to deal effectively with these negative onslaughts is one who has a wide and expanding number of categories in which to file experiences and who can thereby afford to be essentially positive about the future. When such people are planning, forecasting, preparing for, or simply thinking about something that they are going to do, they are confident for two reasons:

1. Since they have had many experiences in the past which have been positive, there is no reason to suspect that the future will be any different.
2. Since they have developed many categories through a variety of experiences, new experiences do not hold a threat of being unable to fit into "the way things are."

Some people are not able to deal with new experiences very well, let alone negative onslaughts. In fact, anything out of the ordinary or unpredictable is potential trouble. Such a view suggests to them that they had better be careful and cautious and expect the worst. After all, that's what the past has been like; why should the future be any different?

Finding and Developing Confidence

In a major study of the lives of more than 200 men over a period of 40 years, researchers at Harvard University have defined some of the characteristics that set apart those people who are able to successfully cope with life from their less successful counterparts. This work, known as the Grant Studies, has recently been published by George Valliant in a book entitled *Adaptation to Life.*[5] Valliant found that for the men in the study the circumstances of their upbringing or occupation had less to do with successful coping than how each one defined his ability to meet challenges head-on and do whatever was necessary to come out on top. In describing methods that people who coped well with their world used, Valliant listed the following:

- Altruism (regard for the interest of others)
- Humor (willingness to see the lighter side)
- Suppression (minimizing of acknowledged discomfort; deliberate postponement, but not avoidance, of conscious impulse and conflict)
- Anticipation (a forward-looking attitude and hopefulness about outcomes of meetings and events)

The *process* by which these men learned to cope successfully was also observed and recorded by Valliant. He identified it as a sequential mastering of one's body, reality (conditions in which we find ourselves), and emotions.

This process of self-discovery is a very different one from that which has been described by others. It emphasizes that one learns most about one's self through association with others. People become more aware of who they are not from *introspection* but from *interaction*—from noticing how they act and react in various situations. This self-knowledge gained through interaction is the key to plotting a determined course toward increased self-confidence.

The Me Decade

This interactive view of self-appraisal is quite a different one from the self-interest approaches recently popularized in books and seminars. It suggests a far different course of action from that taken by 16,000 people who crowded into the Cow Palace in San Francisco to hear Werner Erhard, the founder of EST, tell them they were "turkeys," "robots," "fools," and worse. Why did they take it, even pay for it? Because they were interested in finding out more about the secret, inner "me."

Tom Wolfe called the seventies the "me decade." What he was describing was a concern that seemed to be widespread among people to know about, think about, and talk about their individual identities. Whether this concern about "who am I" is rooted in fad or substance is still to be seen. It is possible to see a kind of pattern developing to approaches that gain popular acceptance and are widely used. Not too long ago self-awareness seemed best gained by attendance at T-groups where participants explored the nature of their feelings with regard to each other. Then came yoga, biofeedback, inner tennis, and transcendental meditation (TM). More recently, jogging, sailing, and mountain climbing have been in vogue. Each method, although different in content, is similar in approach. Each suggests that people learn about themselves by more clearly and closely examining themselves. Although introspection is a part of the process of gaining self-insight, it is only one step along the path and neither the only step necessary nor the destination. It is valuable because it opens other doors.

All people are "in process." We are not fixed entities, but, rather, we are each dynamic individuals who are continuously changing. People are only deluding themselves when they say that they are set in their ways and cannot change or when they say that they are beset by so many obligations that they have almost no autonomy. Most of the time when we say "can't," we really "won't" or "don't" want to," but we say "can't" so often that we come to believe it ourselves. Actually we have many choices, and it is through our choices that we take charge of ourselves. Only when we decide do we define who we are.

By making choices we see opportunities for personal growth. It is seldom easy to choose, to decide. Yet, the process of choosing, itself, produces the kind of growth that makes life worthwhile. By successfully accomplishing difficult tasks, we develop our self-confidence. For some, however, they set such unrealistic goals that they doom themselves to failure. By starting with small tasks and then working up to major goals, we are more likely not only to be successful, but also to feel better about ourselves. Here are some other specific things a person can do to increase self-confidence.

Picking a Model

Much of what we do stems from models whom we have chosen to pattern ourselves after. Sometimes we have consciously chosen to imitate someone else; at other times, we have unconsciously acquired traits or habits from another. A teacher once said that he became a "sun sneezer"—someone who sneezes when walking out of a building into the sunlight—as a result of a respected colleague who said that he always sneezed when walking out of a shaded area into the sunlight.

We probably have different models for the different relationships in our lives. Each of these models has a powerful influence upon us, but most of the time we do not consciously seek out models who represent attributes which we would like to emulate. Consciously picking a model and noticing what things the person does and how she or he goes about doing these things can increase your personal power—provided you select a good model. Observe your model in everyday circumstances, for several weeks, if that is possible, and try to record how the person goes about doing things.

Acting "As If"

The story is told of a timid man named Bunker Bean who visited a gypsy in order to discover his destiny. The gypsy told Bunker Bean that he had many exciting lives to lead in the future just as he had led many in the past. Bunker was told that in a previous life he had been the powerful Napoleon and that he had been instrumental in vanquishing nations. Inspired by such a tale of his past, Bunker Bean decided that he was not going to let his personal heritage down. So he studied Napoleon's tactics and strategies and used them to transform himself into a successful businessman.

Self-fulfilling prophecies can be positive or negative, as we have seen. We can make them about ourselves, others, or even events. Being aware of the events, people, or things which cause us to formulate a self-fulfilling prophecy, and then noticing the prophecy's impact, can be very useful because we can then begin to manage this whole process better. Try spending some specific period of time, say a week or a month, noticing how often you hear yourself or others make an interpersonal self-fulfilling prophecy. If possible, find out if things did turn out as expected. Be sure to include prophecies about such everyday things as meetings, reports, projects, conferences, moods, and customers.

Observing Pygmalion

Since our expectations manifest themselves in subtle ways, of which we are often unaware, learning the ways we communicate to others can be very important. One way to learn this is to observe other people's reactions to things which we say or do. Observing the impact we have on others rather than simply being satisfied with the logic of the words we speak is a necessary step in the positive use of self-fulfilling prophecies. Are other people confused, angry, upset, or eager when you delegate to them? Are meetings productive, inefficient, or a waste of time? Are assignments generally completed on time, or done poorly? One of the consistent findings of managerial research is that nearly all behavior, good and bad, productive and inefficient, is a function of interactions between people and not just one person's "personality." Thus, spending time observing the consequences we produce in others can be extremely useful.

Start keeping a written record of the reactions you tend to produce in others. What things do you do which seem to suggest to others that they can handle an assignment, write a difficult report, or meet a deadline?

What things do you do which suggest the opposite? Remember, base your assessment of such actions on the impact you actually do have and not merely the intentions you may hold.

Displaying Confidence in Employees

The idea of a self-fulfilling prophecy is based on the observation that managers who have confidence in themselves and confidence in others are more effective. How you can personally gain more confidence and how you can build it in others are the subjects of this book. Some guidelines are given and some principles are discussed, but they are not intended to be all-inclusive. The people you work with can also be a good source for this valuable information. What things would they include as ways by which you communicate your expectations of them? What would they say regarding existing goals, policies, and procedures? You'll never know unless you ask them. Moreover, by asking them you will communicate that you think enough of their opinions and judgment to seek out their points of view. This action in itself is one way to begin to communicate high regard and positive expectations.

High Self-Esteem Required for Managerial Effectiveness

It should be apparent that the idea of self-esteem and the need for individuals to continually confirm their view of themselves may help to explain some important aspects of organizational behavior. First, task requirements must demand much of people in the way of skill and knowledge, not just output, if a high sense of personal worth and competence is going to be affirmed by people on the job. Thus, if a manager or some other employee is motivated by a desire to demonstrate competence to himself or herself and others, but is in a job that does not allow this, the person's response to the job may well become one of apathy. Many jobs expect too little of people, and so the employees pour their energy into hobbies and other avocational pursuits.

Second, a sense of personal worth is not measured by any absolute scale. Instead it depends to a large degree on feedback from people and events in a person's surroundings. A quarterback who throws a "bomb" for a touchdown is given immediate feedback both by seeing a teammate catch the ball and cross the goal line, and by hearing the confirming roar of approval from supporters. But can you imagine how it would feel if no one cheered, not even the person's teammates? The quarterback would probably wonder if a touchdown pass had indeed been thrown. For people in such positions feelings of personal worth and success are strongly influenced by the behavior of others toward them.

This is also true in a work setting. People experience increases in self-esteem primarily from the work environment, through feedback. This feedback comes from two sources: a personal evaluation of achievement on a task and a communicated appraisal conveyed by others. This explains one of the conditions which probably were operating in the famous Western Electric studies. What had been a routine and unexciting job became more appealing because work methods and outputs were being observed and analyzed by a team of behavioral scientists. Almost overnight a rather dull job was transformed into one capable of providing employees with feelings of personal worth and competence. The result was an increase in worker productivity.

Summary

The process of accumulating data on life's experiences and categorizing them appears to be essentially the same for everyone. Yet, even though the process is the same, the end product is very different depending largely on how we see ourselves. So changing how people see themselves is the real key to their personal development and the basis for effective interpersonal functioning.

One of the more consistent findings of managerial research is that nearly all behavior—good and bad, productive and unproductive—is a function of interactions between people and not just a person's "personality." This is not to say that we don't each have an individual personality, but rather that our personality is largely shaped by the interactions we have. We all seem to learn who we are and what to do mainly from an accumulation of contacts and experiences with other people. Harry Stack Sullivan, one of America's most prominent psychologists, called this development "learning about self from the mirror of other people."[6] Thus, what people believe about themselves is based partly on their interpretation of how significant others in their lives see them. Since we really have no way of knowing how other people see us, we make inferences based on their behavior toward us. As an old adage goes, we are what we think other people think we are.

Our view of ourselves, then, is dramatically influenced by two factors: 1) our feelings of success in the past and anticipation of those successes in the future and 2) our perception of how the people who count regard us. These two factors are like sparkplugs which determine how well a person performs in most social situations. This view of ourselves is flexible and changes from situation to situation depending on what role we think others are expecting us to perform and how competent we feel in the role we decide upon. Thus, we may feel confident and competent as a parent but not as a scout leader. Or we may feel in control at a staff meeting but unsure or hesitant at a civic club meeting. Moreover, we may feel that we can adequately explain the recommendations contained in a report to our boss but feel inadequate to do the same thing for our boss's boss. Our view of ourselves changes in a variety of settings and can be changed, by intent, in a variety of ways. We can feel more confident, more competent, more in control, and thereby more productive and effective through determined effort and by structuring a nourishing environment.

Since events and people have a significant impact on you in ways which you cannot always control, one key to feeling better about yourself is to structure your environment so that you get what you want. This means creating successful experiences and positive interactions for yourself. Who are the people you know who are important to you and who believe in your abilities? You can contract with them to critique your performance on various projects and thereby get some specific feedback on how these significant people in your life actually regard the work you do. What are the things you do well, your own special skills and abilities? Leading from strength can enable you to get better and better at whatever you do.

References

1. Gardner, B. B.: *What Makes Successful and Unsuccessful Executives?* (New York: Society for the Advancement of Management, 1948).
2. Coopersmith, Stanley: *The Antecedents of Self-Esteem* (San Francisco: Freeman, 1967).
3. Zaleznick, Abraham, and David G. Moment: *Dynamics of Interpersonal Behavior* (New York: Wiley, 1964).
4. Zaleznick, Abraham, Louis Barnes, and Gene W. Dalton: *Orientation and Conflict in Careers* (Cambridge, Mass.: Harvard University Press, 1970).
5. Valliant, George: *Adaptation to Life* (New York: Little, Brown, 1979).
6. Sullivan, Harry S.: *Clinical Studies in Psychiatry* (New York: Norton, 1973).

Chapter 3

Beliefs, Symbols, and Words

I am successful. I am beautiful. I am quiet. I am assertive. I am a homebody. I am a natural athlete.

I am sensitive. I am funny. I am insecure. I am musically inclined. I handle pressure well.

I am dissatisfied. I can't do two things at once. I am not that kind of woman. I get emotional easily.

I am rebellious. I am practical. I am an ordinary guy. I am uneducated. I am just a country boy.

Which of these phrases describe you? Draw a circle around each which describes you most of the time. All such statements are more or less accurate "maps" of that "territory" which is ourselves. Some people make better maps to describe themselves than others do. If we make a reasonably accurate map of ourselves—our strengths and weaknesses—this self-assessment is a significant prop to our self-esteem because the words we use to *describe* who we are *affect* our belief about who we are. What we do, how we dress, what mannerisms we adopt, what tasks we choose to undertake or avoid, what goals we set, what activities we try are

31

determined not so much by our *actual* background, abilities, and limitations as by what we *believe* our background, abilities, and limitations are. We tend to unconsciously think, "What should someone like me be like?" and we act accordingly. Office workers who do not act as the society within their organization says they should may be labeled as "unprofessional."

However, a "map" is not a "territory"—it is only an approximation and may be accurate or inaccurate depending upon the skills of the map maker. So, our evaluation of ourselves may or may not be accurate depending on our individual skills and abilities at self-evaluation. Just as even the best of maps omit an enormous amount of terrain, so one's self-evaluation can delete significant portions of potential and ability. We can *describe* ourselves to ourselves and then make any number of *inferences* and *generalizations* which may or may not be realistic depending upon the accuracy of our data gathering and the thoroughness of our conclusions.

How we choose to describe ourselves, not just in the exercise at the beginning of this chapter but in everyday experience, can powerfully affect our actions. Sometimes words can use us as much as we use them. Notice the difference between such phrases as the following:

> I have failed three times (which is a report, suggesting mistakes are natural and nothing to be concerned about).
>
> I am a failure (which is a judgment, suggesting mistakes are all one makes).
>
> I am a supervisor (which is a report, simply a description).
>
> I am only a supervisor (which is a judgment, implying that one should be something different).

The pitfalls of map-territory relations—of description-generalization—therefore may threaten the adequacy of our evaluations of ourselves as well as of other people. As the proliferation of psychologists, counselors, and others in the personal helping profession demonstrates, we all seem to have ways from time to time of concealing deep and yet basic parts of ourselves from ourselves and others. We often justify our actions after the fact and develop rationalizations to protect ourselves from too much self-evaluation. It's much easier that way.

Self-knowledge, of course, is often painful. It is not easy to say "My real reason for feeling angry that she got a promotion is because I'm jealous of her. I'm just not as intelligent as she is." It may be much easier to pass off disappointment over not being promoted in such an instance with a remark such as "I guess a pretty face and nice legs is what it takes to get ahead around here." How do we prevent ourselves from getting into the kind of emotional predicaments where we continually rationalize our actions or conditions that exist in our lives? One of the most important things that we can do is avoid passing judgment on ourselves.

The fact that we permit other people's judgments (and what we *believe* their judgments to be) to influence us unduly is one of the most common reasons for insecurity and lack of achievement. I have a friend who is good and capable and intelligent. He is also black. To me, the fact that his skin is black does nothing more to me than the fact that my eyes are blue. But he has accepted the judgment he *believes* most white people make about all blacks and may spend the rest of his life being defensive and suspicious and miserable. This evaluation of what he thinks others believe has seriously affected his ability to process information accurately. He is less able to make choices freely and decide whom he can trust and whom he cannot because of his predetermined evaluation. Of course, he has had enough experiences to suggest that his conclusion is not wholly unwarranted.

Since the source of many problems in our self-evaluation process is the clouding of our description of events with unwarranted judgments, perhaps an exercise in separating event from its perception would be useful. Take a piece of paper and write down as many facts as you can about yourself. Include, if you will, characteristics which cause you to feel some twinge of remorse or even embarrassment. Then, ask yourself the following series of questions:

- Is this a fact or an evaluation?
- How do I know it is an accurate description of a personal strength or weakness? Who says?
- Should I agree with the assessment of me by others?
- So what? What difference does agreement or disagreement make?
- Am I different today in that area from what I was in the past?

The more we are able to describe our feelings and confront our beliefs about things that have occurred in our past, the more likely we are to make accurate self-evaluations. As we accept ourselves in this manner, we can accept without evaluating as *good* or *bad* such descriptions about ourselves as "I am shorter than the average male," "I am taller than the average female," "I am not mechanically inclined," "I am not athletic." We have less and less need to deceive ourselves and are better able to choose for ourselves the kind of person we want to be. We progressively move to the conquest of more difficult areas, and thus we enhance our ability as we increase our awareness.

Nonverbal Cues and How They Influence Us

People orient themselves to their world through cues they receive from their immediate environment. Such cues are both spoken and unspoken messages about "how things should be done." We construct symbols and establish rituals to identify the status, position, and roles of people particularly in the organizations to which we belong. This can be most readily observed in fraternities and sororities, where status and ritual are obvious, as well as a daily governing influence. Perhaps no one has studied such influence as much as Erving Goffman, a longtime professor of sociology at the University of Pennsylvania.

He has observed that people have a sense of "personal territoriality." This includes certain personal rights one assumes are valid, such as the right not to be touched and not to be dragged into a stranger's conversation, and the right to informational privacy—which partly refers to the questions one doesn't expect to be asked. The average American, for example, would be insulted by questions concerning personal income or sex life if asked by a casual acquaintance, though in some cultures these are considered perfectly polite questions to ask. Likewise, most Americans would be angry if someone tried to read their mail or go through their wallet or dig too deeply into their personal background. The typical American's need for informational privacy extends even to appearance and details of behavior, for most people also believe they have a right not to be stared at.

As always, where there are rules of order, there are ways of breaking them, of intruding: by physical invasion of another's space, by touching what one has no "right" to touch, by staring, by making more noise than the occasion warrants, or by making uncalled-for remarks—for example, the remarks of a subordinate who speaks out of turn, or of a stranger who breaks into a private conversation, or of a panhandler who approaches a passerby on the street.

Events are always arising in public life that give the impression that some intrusion has occurred, and there's a considerable amount of daily ritual that has to be gone through to nullify these impressions. When we bump into someone, we apologize; caught staring, we hastily look away. In cases of self-intrusion, onlookers are expected to play their part. We are not supposed to notice when other people pick their noses or come unzipped. And if forced to overhear someone else's conversation, one is expected to behave as though deaf. It's often quite easy in public to eavesdrop on a conversation, but when people do, they invariably try to conceal the fact that they're listening. Imagine what would happen if the listener candidly watched those who were conversing and joined in.

There's one situation in which the territories of the self are deliberately and systematically invaded—during encounter groups. Encounter participants are urged to stare at each other, to touch one another, to ask and answer intimate questions, and to share their honest emotions, particularly the socially unacceptable ones. Most of these behaviors are taken for granted between lovers and even, up to a point, between good friends. But in an encounter group, it's strangers who share the trappings of intimacy, apparently in the hope that deeply emotional, even if temporary, relationships will result.

That we all have a mask—a face—that we present to the world is a point Goffman made in his book *Interaction Ritual*.[1] And we try hard to save face when necessary in order to preserve the impression that we're capable and strong and to avoid looking foolish. We're concerned about preserving not only our own public image but also those of other people. This means that the role chosen by each member of a group is usually accepted by the other members. If two people who have just broken up turn up unexpectedly at the same party and decide to pretend theirs was a civilized parting—though it wasn't—bystanders will, with great relief, cooperate in the charade. For if one person commits a faux pas, everyone's equilibrium is simultaneously threatened and must be restored.

People often cooperate in mutual face-saving in intricate and subtle ways, and this kind of face-saving is at its most fascinating when it comes to one-to-one relationships. Goffman has observed that in the beginning of any friendship, particularly a male-female one, both persons are supposed to demonstrate that they're not too readily available. At the same time, they have to get on with developing the relationship, and so all this must be managed by signs, and not too obvious ones at that. These signs tip the other person off to what's likely to happen so that, as a by-product, each can save a little face if necessary. Especially in courtship, each person wants to avoid being put in a position of being openly rejected or of rejecting the other person.

Sometimes when a situation shows us up in a bad light, to save face we go about providing a correction for it in words or gestures. When the situation is minor and occurs in public, so that it's not really possible to address an explanation directly to any of the strangers present, we're more likely to use a broad, self-conscious gesture, what Goffman calls "body gloss."

For example, a person leafing through an "adult" magazine in a store may take care to flip the pages fairly rapidly, so as to give the impression of simply looking for a particular article to anyone watching. If an abandoned parcel is occupying a chair someone would like to sit in, that person will show that he or she is merely moving it and has no designs on it by handling it by the edges in a gingerly fashion. People who blunder into a supposedly empty room only to find a meeting in progress often screw up their faces and contract their upper bodies as they quietly withdraw and ease the door shut behind them; as Goffman says, they manage "to tiptoe . . . face and upper trunk."[2] And if someone is leaning against a wall, taking up sidewalk space, and another person approaches, the leaner is very likely to do a "loller's tuck"—, that is, pull in and back, however subtly, as the other draws abreast, as if to make room or at any rate to indicate the will to make room.

The point demonstrated by all this is that no one is ever really alone and anonymous in a crowd; nor do people simply move mechanically from place to place. Whenever they're out in public, they constantly and half deliberately behave so as to provide evidence of good character. Though a person may seem totally indifferent to people all around, these people are, potentially, the audience, and the person the actor, if a situation arises that threatens compromise.

Any face-to-face relationship except perhaps the most fleeting tends to seek its own equilibrium. Matters such as the relative status of the participants, the degree of intimacy they're going to express, what roles they're going to play, and what topics are suitable for discussion are sorted out until there is some kind of shared unspoken agreement. Most often, the sorting out is done even before the people come together, so that when they meet, they already know where they stand—if a man runs into his brother-in-law on the street, it's usually unnecessary for them to renegotiate their relationship. The kind of conversation a woman has with the mail carrier is unlike the kind she has with her mother, and in each case the situation—the role each will play—is pretty well predefined.

Symbols and How They Influence Us

Language and the use of words is essentially a symbolic process. Words are used to represent things which exist, but sometimes these words are confused with the thing they are intended to symbolize. Like the child who said, "Pigs are called pigs because they are such dirty animals," we all tend sometimes to confuse words and things.

So it is with our description of ourselves. The words which we or others use do not necessarily accurately describe who we are or what we can do. Still, the symbol, like all symbols, powerfully affects us. For whatever people believe to be true either is true or becomes true in their minds. As Susanne Langer, a noted psychologist, has observed: "The symbol making function is one of man's primary activities, like eating, looking or moving about. It is a fundamental process of the mind and goes on all of the time."[3]

Symbols can affect how we think about ourselves in a variety of ways. They can certainly control actions. For instance people desiring a break with the past will often go through a "housecleaning" phase. They want to eliminate past memories, and so they destroy the symbols which suggest them.

Symbols are the integrating factors of life. We do, after all, work for symbols. Status, recognition, even money, carry symbolic messages of success and achievement. Advertisers in particular recognize this symbol-making perspective of humankind and attempt to manipulate symbols to induce buying behavior.

Most people surround themselves with a variety of symbols that are emotionally meaningful. Pictures in a photograph album, souvenirs from a vacation, gifts from trusted friends all suggest past pleasures and future hopes. Objects which have very positive emotional meanings can be specifically created and used to build the confidence and enhance the competence of others.

This is essentially what David McClelland, a Harvard psychologist, has done in training business people working in foreign countries. McClelland structures activities for participants in his training course so they will talk, think, and then act like a person with a high achievement goal. The more symbols of achievement people can be supplied with, the more likely they are to live up to their essential characteristics. In essence, this is another adaption of the self-fulfilling prophecy.

In his writings, McClelland illustrates the importance of this symbol-creating process with this tale.[4] It seems there was once a certain medieval king who wanted to know his chances in a forthcoming battle. He went to a local soothsayer who was noted for accuracy in making predictions and asked the seer's opinion on the fray. The soothsayer replied that the king would be victorious as long as he did not think about the left eye of a camel. The end of the tale is that the king lost the battle because he could not, of course, refrain from thinking about the camel's left eye. Now if the king were told simply to avoid *looking* at the left eye of a camel, that would have been easy. But the suggestion, once planted, could not be avoided regardless of the consequences.

Symbols motivate people to act differently because they think of themselves in different lights. Symbols can cause people to "reframe"—or look from a different frame of reference at—their previous experiences and to see themselves differently. Again, the work of David McClelland has forcefully demonstrated the salience of this observation.[5] McClelland has written that all motives—stimulants to act—are learned. These motives develop as a result of significant emotional events which cause us to regard and believe and feel about things as we do. We associate emotional reactions and conjure up images in our minds to generalize about these experiences and tie them to everyday life. As long as the way we label our experiences continues, we remain unchanged in our belief about our capabilities. Thus, successful experiences will not improve our self-evaluation unless we also learn to recognize our achievements and give ourselves credit for them. Of course, this also extends to other people who are important to us: without their recognition of our achievements we are likely to depreciate them ourselves. We might pass them off with statements like "Aw, anyone could do (or would have done) it in the same circumstance" or "I guess I got a lucky break. It was being in the right place at the right time that mattered, not my ability."

McClelland has spent years teaching managers how to develop a heightened achievement motive and has articulated a process for doing so. The first procedure, he maintains, is to create confidence in the participants that the methods really work. It seems that the more reasons people have for believing that taking a specific course of action will yield certain desirable results, the more likely they are to take such action. We don't want to waste our time on something that won't work. Consequently, we work hard to have things in which we invest a lot of time and energy "turn out right"—the self-fulfilling prophecy.

The next step is to tie thought to action. Since McClelland's research has shown that people who are achievers prefer work situations where there is a challenge; concrete feedback on specific, well-defined goals; and opportunity to take personal responsibility for those goals, he has tried to develop these characteristics in his training programs. The more people both *think* and *act* as achievers, the more likely they are to develop this trait.

This is obviously more than "think and grow rich" or the "power of positive thinking." What we believe about ourselves, the words we use to describe the person that we are, and the image that we have about ourselves are all important and exert a powerful influence in our day-to-day lives. However, we do not fashion these images and create expectations about our behavior all by ourselves. We are, instead, heavily influenced by those whose opinions we value and by our prior experiences. We seldom are able to put such influences easily aside. The simple faith which Maxwell Maltz, Clement Stone, and others who have written on the psychology of self-esteem place in the almost limitless plasticity of human behavior is revealing. Are we really so rootless and easily influenced as they suggest? Can something which takes little effort produce great strength? The physical sciences suggest that strength is forged, not simply claimed. The behavioral sciences, if studied carefully, provide the same conclusion. We can change. It is not necessarily a long-drawn-out process. But it is certainly an *intense* one, causing us to re-examine what we believe and how we act.

Words and How They Influence Us

A considerable interest in the processes of communication has been generated in recent years—especially among managers. Courses in interpersonal communications abound. One manufacturing firm even ran a national television advertisement extolling the benefits of a program they developed for their employees on the subject. Despite this interest, little has been done in the way of looking at communication to see how the words we use shape our beliefs in others as well as in ourselves.

It has been said that words use us as much as we use them. The range of means we have to describe events or thoughts or feelings inhibits or enhances our ability to understand something fully. It is not surprising that an eskimo has more than 150 different words for snow or that in most American Indian dialects there is no word for "time" and only general means for describing its passage. Words are more than a means for expression. They shape what we know and believe to be true, because of the images they create.

It is possible that any person who works in an organization can learn more about how to assess and improve its overall effectiveness by first understanding and then attempting to change the images or metaphors that people use to describe their workaday lives there. For instance, if a manager were to ask people to suggest anonymous analogies for the organization, what would they say? Would the analogies be to TV's M*A*S*H unit, where those on the firing line continually needed to circumvent rules and regulations to get things done? Would they be to a monarch and the royal court? Or a flea market where no one really knows what's going on?

Words are more than just sounds we use to convey a message. They reflect the personality and the environment of the person speaking as well. They are in effect a mirror of the kind of person we think we are. The words we use reinforce our position of status as well as our feelings and beliefs. The upwardly mobile person uses "in" words, aggressive phrases, apt descriptions, while the indifferent person uses noncompetitive words, and the anxious person uses ambivalent phrases. Further, words not only mean different things to different people but also carry different degrees of meaning. The 500 most used words (according to Thorndyke's Word Book) have over 12,078 separate and distinct definitions in the Oxford English Dictionary.

Although we continually strive to make ourselves understood, our efforts are not always successful. We may suppose that we need to be more articulate or analytical or even self-effacing. Maybe. Maybe, however, we need to examine what our words say about us and the confidence with which we communicate the suggestions we make to others.

Summary

Most people surround themselves with a variety of symbols that are emotionally meaningful. Objects that have very positive emotional meanings can be selected or specifically created. Symbols that relate to your ideals, values, and goals can be employed to help you do what you want to do.

In any organization of appreciable size there are hierarchies that divide responsibility by position. This can create a special problem for aspiring junior executives and even middle managers, who may face a "destination crisis." They believe that they must occupy a certain place within the organization by a certain time in their life. If they don't "arrive" on time, they may be more than disappointed. They may demand modification and revision. Whether they emerge as cynical or resilient from such a process can be influenced by those around them if others are sensitive to pertinent events as they occur. Alterations in beliefs, symbols, or words may be signals as well as targets of personal change.

References

1. Goffman, Erving: *Interaction Ritual: Essays in Face-to-Face Behavior* (New York: Pantheon, 1982).
2. Goffman, Erving: *Frame Analysis: An Essay on the Organization of Experience* (Cambridge, Mass.: Harvard University Press, 1974).
3. Langer, Susanne K.: *Philosophy in a New Key: A Study in the Symbolism of Reason, Rite, and Art* (Cambridge, Mass.: Harvard University Press, 1957).
4. McClelland, David C.: *Power: The Inner Experience* (New York: Irvington, 1979).
5. McClelland, David C.: *The Achieving Society* (New York: Van Nostrand, 1961).

Part II

Interpersonal Processes

Chapter 4

Self-Esteem and the Self-Fulfilling Prophecy in Management

In everything we do or fail to do, we communicate attitudes and values that others take as cues to their own behavior. The extent to which the positions we project are picked up by others, however, depends largely on the confidence people sense we have in ourselves and in our point of view. Our communicated attitudes and expectations act as self-fulfilling prophecies when we really believe in them ourselves.

This notion of a self-fulfilling prophecy based on attitudes and expectations has long been recognized by behavioral scientists, therapists, and doctors. The existing evidence for the effects of these interpersonal self-fulfilling prophecies is almost overwhelming. Yet, these findings have not been widely communicated nor the implications for action generally understood.

The findings of these researchers have some clear implications for managers. The research suggests that what confident managers expect of those they supervise significantly affects employee performance. If managers' actions communicate that they have high, but realistic, performance expectations, it has the effect on employees of setting up a target that they want to reach. But if managerial actions communicate low expectations, no such incentive will be created.

These findings regarding managing through confident action and the creation of positive expectations which others want to fulfill point to a management style that is needed today. In recent years, the dilemma of an appropriate management style has put many managers between the "rock" of excessive permissiveness and the "hard place" of unacceptable authoritarianism. Placed in this quandary between giving in too much and being too strict, many managers have vacillated between the two and left others seeing them as wishy-washy.

There is a new balance that is needed between supervisor and supervised. Most people want certainty in their lives and are willing to go to great lengths to make those who are close to them predictable. This natural tendency partially explains why the self-fulfilling prophecy works. We do not like to be surprised.

An ordinary example illustrates this. When we are led to expect that we are about to meet a pleasant person, our amicable behavior based on our expectations at this first meeting may, in fact, make the person more pleasant. But if we are led to expect someone unpleasant, our approach may be so defensive at our meeting that we make the person behave unpleasantly toward us.

A high school principal put this idea to a test one year to see if it really worked. Throughout the school year as substitute teachers were needed in various classrooms, he would distribute biographies of the new teachers before their arrival. The biographies were identical except that they described half the substitutes as "warm, concerned, and supportive" and half as "cold, rigid, and demanding." Substantial differences resulted in the students' subsequent evaluations of the teachers and in their interaction patterns with them. The students who expected the substitutes to be warm and supportive rated them higher as effective teachers and interacted with them frequently. Those who were led to believe that their substitutes would be cold and rigid had less to do with them and rated them as being poor.

What people believe that important other people think of them powerfully affects their self-image. This certainly includes family and friends as well as coworkers and supervisors. Since supervisors and managers have the authority to alter a person's status at the workplace, they can dramatically affect a person's self-image. Rare is the person who can be productive and maintain self-esteem when treated poorly by supervisors and others at work.

This was the point George Bernard Shaw was trying to make when he wrote the play *Pygmalion*, the basis for the musical hit *My Fair Lady*. In the play, Shaw describes how Professor Higgins, an expert in languages and dialects, takes a London flower girl out of poverty and within a matter of months is able to pass her off at a celebrity ball as a princess.

Near the conclusion of the story, the girl, Eliza Doolittle, explains to Higgins's mother the reason for her development. It was not result of the professor's teaching ability, but of Mrs. Higgins's belief in Eliza. Eliza explains it this way:

> You see, really and truly, apart from the things anyone can pick up—the dressing and the proper way of speaking; and so on—the difference between a lady and a flower girl is not how she behaves, but how she's treated. I shall always be a flower girl to Professor Higgins, because he always treats me as a flower girl, and always will; but I know I can be a lady to you, because you always treat me as a lady and always will.

This operation of a self-fulfilling prophecy, or the Pygmalion effect as it is sometimes called, based on expectations and the subsequent treatment of others, goes in both directions. That is, people tend to fulfill the expectations of others regardless of whether they are positive or not.

Every organization, every manager provides people with a sense of what is expected of them. If the expectations are sparse or lax, then people will exert little effort. If the expectations are negative, then people will be submissive, but act out what they think is "really" expected of them. However, if much is expected of employees in an organization, then chances are that people will expect much of themselves. It is possible to create an atmosphere that encourages effort, striving, and vigorous performance. It is possible to establish a climate where people want to fulfill the expectations of those who guide and direct them.

The importance of creating high-performance expectations has been suggested as a critical factor which distinguishes high-producing organizational units from low-producing units by Rensis Likert, founder of the Institute for Social Research at the University of Michigan. After two decades of research, Likert concluded that managers could use any number of motivational programs and get either no return or a negative return from their time and money investment. What did make a difference in motivation and productivity, Likert discovered, was a manager's expectations of employees' performance.

The concept of how a manager's expectations influence an employee's performance is dramatically illustrated in the case of "Sweeney's miracle." James Sweeney taught industrial management and psychiatry at Tulane University in the mid 1960s. He was also responsible for the operation and administration of the university's biomedical computer center. In his capacity as administrator, Sweeney directed a staff of people ranging from data programmers to maintenance workers. It was Sweeney's expectation that he could convert a poorly educated black janitor into a competent computer operator. So he talked to George Johnson, a janitor at the computer center, and convinced Johnson to spend his free afternoons learning about computers. Johnson was learning a great deal about computers when a university administration official approached Sweeney and indicated that there was a requirement that all operators pass an IQ test before being allowed into the center. Johnson took the test and flunked. His test results indicated that he did not have the capacity to learn to type, much less to program a computer. Still, Sweeney was convinced of his own ability to teach Johnson to run a computer. He went to the university administration and convinced the administrators to let Johnson stay on and promised them that he would show some positive results from his efforts. Within months Johnson was so proficient at programming that he was asked to train new employees in the operation of the center.

Sweeney's miracle was not the first time that the self-fulfilling prophecy was observed in the world of work. In 1890 a new type of tabulating machine known as the Hollerith was installed in various locations at the Bureau of the Census. The new equipment, similar to a typewriter, required the clerks to learn a new skill. The inventor of the machine, Hollerith, regarded the skill as quite demanding and expected that a trained worker could punch about 550 cards a day. After about 2 weeks, when the workers had completed their training, they began to produce at the expected rate of 550 cards per day. During the next few months some of the workers began to exceed the expected performance amount but became so tense and upset that they were discouraged from doing so by the secretary of the interior.

Then a new group of about 200 clerks was employed who knew nothing about the Hollerith machine and had no knowledge of the previous standards. They were trained and assigned to separate locations from the previous group of employees. No expected performance standard was communicated except that the employees were encouraged to do all that they could. Within 3 days this new group was producing at the top level reached by their predecessors. Whereas the earlier group was exhausted if they turned out 700 cards per day, the new group did two or three times that number with no apparent side effects. They did not have a limiting expectation, and so they were able to do more than the initial group of workers.

Although it is important for managers to establish and communicate high performance expectations in order to reap their benefits, it is not an easy task to do. In fact, the things we consciously do will have no impact if they are not congruent with the things we unconsciously do. It is the things we do of which we are hardly aware that often communicate what we expect of others. Somehow, regardless of many of the things we may overtly do or say, what we really believe comes through.

In other words, our attitude shows. Our attitude reflects in the way we do things and profoundly affects the impact we have on others. A prominent management writer, Douglas MacGregor, maintains that our attitude—or what he calls the assumptions we make about human nature—is the determinant of a manager's influence upon others. MacGregor maintains that if a manager believes that her or his employees are lazy, don't want to work, and lack ambition, yet tells them something quite different, they will not believe the person's words. For instance, if a manager delegates a project to an employee with the words "I really trust you and know you can handle it," but then requires the employee to get authorization from the manager before making any decision regarding the project, the employee will realize that the verbal expression of trust is hollow.

A manager's negative or low expectations of a particular employee's performance always shine through because the actions which communicate most are often the ones the manager is aware of least. Positive expectations, on the other hand, are difficult for managers to communicate and to use as a method that is part of their managerial style because they require the mastery of some specific skills in order to be accurately conveyed. While these skills can be learned, their effective use depends on two crucial factors:

- A manager's self-confidence and confidence in his or her own abilities
- A manager's belief in the ability of those he or she supervises

These two factors indicate that the positive effects of a self-fulfilling prophecy are not available to the cynical manipulator. This is because the things we expect actually reflect what we believe about ourselves and others and must complement what we do in order for desirable results to be obtained. What managers do must be consistent with what they believe in order for a positive impact to result.

This was demonstrated several years ago when a group of managers attended a leadership training course. The seminar was geared to acquainting them with the research evidence regarding interpersonal self-fulfilling prophecies and to practicing skills that communicated positive expectations to others. A review of the evidence was included in order to convince the managers of the utility of using the skills that were also to be taught. Several of those who attended saw this idea as a gimmick that they could apply to get better performance from those they supervised, without making any changes in themselves. Not only did these managers not experience the increased results they had hoped for, but some even experienced negative effects. Employees in these units became resentful of the unrealistic quotas which were imposed on them and of the insincerity of their bosses. Turnover and absenteeism increased, while productivity declined.

What we believe counts as much as what we do when it comes to self-fulfilling prophecies. The things which we often don't realize that we do generally come through louder and clearer than one might expect. This is amply illustrated by an incident which occurred at approximately the turn of the century in Germany. It is about a horse known as Clever Hans.

Horse Sense

Van Osten, the owner of Clever Hans, was a school teacher who was curious about the possibility of teaching animals how to answer arithmetic problems. He began to teach his horse every evening to tap out, with one of his hooves, answers to problems that would be presented to him. Hans became so good at clopping out just the right number of strokes in order to have the correct answer that his owner began to exhibit him at local fairs. For any problem that was given to him, including algebraic equations, Hans invariably tapped out the correct solution. In fact, he could get right answers that even required him to read and to spell. Hans's ability became so well known that a state-appointed commission was organized to investigate Van Osten and the purported ability of his horse to think rationally and compute numbers correctly. In order to determine whether or not Van Osten was giving Hans some kind of sign to begin and to stop tapping, the commission prohibited Hans's owner from being present while they investigated. One by one the commissioners would whisper a complex arithmetic problem into Hans's ear, and one by one they were amazed to find that Hans could tap out the correct answer.

Of course, Hans's fame spread when the results of the commission were known. Still, there were skeptics, and within a few months another commission investigated Van Osten's claims. This commission, after a series of extraordinary experiments, reversed the position of the earlier investigative body. They found that Hans could only answer questions when the questioners themselves knew the right answer. Hans was able to detect subtle cues from the questioners, a tiny forward motion of the head to start and a raised eyebrow or inaudible sign to stop, and was thereby able to get the right answer. Surprisingly, even when questioners knew that they were giving Hans silent cues, they could not prevent themselves from displaying them. Such unconscious cues were, in this case, impossible to consciously control.

The expectations of those who questioned Hans affected their behavior in ways of which they were completely unaware. Interestingly, their expectations were communicated in their unwilling signals to stop and start tapping. Clever Hans was a sensitive observer—and a smart horse.

The implications of this incident are great and essentially mean that if we really want to understand what goes on between people and how a manager can positively influence others, we must concentrate on nonverbal responses. This means that besides the nonverbal messages which we send to others, we must be aware of their nonverbal responses back to us. Words are only a part of communication along with nonverbal messages and nonverbal responses.

Communication can best be understood as a system wherein all parts—verbal and nonverbal—are related and influence one another. To better understand interpersonal behavior, we must look at ongoing patterns and not just at isolated pieces of a message. We are always communicating and we are always influencing the behavior of others around us. Thus, we are, in part, both molding the behavior of others through our expectations and actions and being molded by others' expectations and actions toward us. The process is interactive.

William F. Whyte, a Cornell researcher, noticed while studying the behavior of people in groups the significant effects of such interactive expectations. Whyte observed the bowling behavior of members of a close-knit group over a considerable period of time. He found that the group, and especially its leaders, "knew" how well a person was going to bowl on a given night. In fact, each person usually performed as expected. On certain nights when the group "knew" that a person was to do well, the person generally did. On other evenings, when supposed to have a bad night, the person usually did, even having bowled well the night before. The group's expectations, and particularly those of the leaders, were a major influence in whether or not each person did well on a particular night.

None of us likes to be proved wrong. Consequently, we will sometimes go to great lengths to be sure that any predictions, silent or otherwise, do in fact come true. Sweeney was convinced of his own ability to teach George Johnson how to run a computer and was unwilling to accept the results of an IQ test which suggested that he might be wrong. Perhaps the encouragement and support offered by those who were seen as leaders on the bowling team to those who were expected to do well on a given night helped them to do so by increasing their motivation and decreasing their anxiety. The confidence of individual group members was enhanced because of their leaders' confidence in them.

The reason that those who possess a high degree of self-confidence are able to influence others in this way is because their own sense of personal security is not violated in interpersonal exchanges. Because of their own positive evaluations of themselves, such people feel neither threat nor insecurity when others do well. In work settings, when such people are supervisors, they are influential because they exhibit the same confidence toward workers with which they regard themselves. Thus, they are able to enhance the self-confidence of other employees and thereby increase such employees' productive capacity.

It is not that such supervisory expectations totally define other workers' self-confidence. But they do define, to a considerable extent, the things most employees feel comfortable doing on the job. In other words, it lets certain people—who say they otherwise wouldn't do it—be assertive, or ask for assistance, or try out a new idea. As one person said, the presence of positive supervisory and managerial expectations "helps me to put on my act, to get my play presented." For many employees, managerial expectations also determine which act to put on, which play to present.

This may explain the success of three formal tests of the self-fulfilling prophecy in industrial settings. In one study, a professor at Kansas State University, Albert King, with no previous knowledge of any shop personnel, randomly picked the names of several welder trainees and told their supervisor that these trainees showed a high aptitude for welding. In fact, King knew nothing of their aptitude or ability. Months later, he found that these workers had learned their jobs faster, produced more in an average day, and were absent fewer times than their peers. Somehow the supervisor of these employees whose names had been picked out of a hat was able to convince them that they could succeed at welding. And succeed they did.

In another study, a large number of female applicants for employment underwent a series of pre-employment tests. The supervisors who were asked to oversee these employees were told that certain of the new hires had done remarkably well on the pre-employment exams, while others had scored quite poorly. In fact, what the supervisors were told had no relationship to the actual performance of the applicants on the exams. After several months, the actual production records of each newly hired person were reviewed. The records indicated that the productivity of those who had been identified as scoring well on the initial exams was substantially higher than that of any of the others, while the records of those who had been identified as scoring poorly on the initial tests showed lower-than-average performance. Interestingly, the workers' actual tests, which were designed to measure intelligence and manual dexterity, showed no relationship to their individual production output. This result could only be interpreted as another case of a self-fulfilling prophecy.

A third test of the effects of an interpersonal self-fulfilling prophecy has been reported by Sterling Livingston, a former professor at the Harvard Business School. Livingston reports that a district manager of a large insurance company put his top performers in the same unit and then assigned them to work under the most capable of the assistant managers in the district. The district manager then asked this group to produce two-thirds of the premium volume achieved by the entire district the year before. The district manager's plan worked. The top agents produced as expected, and the overall district's performance improved about 40 percent. Although the productivity of these agents did improve dramatically and stayed at high levels, the performance of those who were not considered to have any chance of reaching a certain sales level actually declined. The district manager's expectations largely determined the performance of his best and his worst agents.

The influence of one person's expectations on another person's behavior is not, of course, a business discovery. In fact, the first observation of this effect appears to have occurred anciently. George Bernard Shaw used *Pygmalion* as the title for his play because of a Greek myth which tells of a king named Pygmalion who carved the statue of a beautiful woman who was subsequently brought to life. Pygmalion's longing for the woman whose image he had carved was so powerful that Aphrodite, goddess of love, brought the statue to life, thereby fulfilling Pygmalion's expectation for such a woman. Thus, as we saw earlier in this chapter, the Pygmalion effect has sometimes been used to describe the self-fulfilling prophecy.

For that reason Robert Rosenthal, a Harvard psychologist, and Lenore Jacobsen, a San Francisco school teacher, entitled their book, which describes the results of experiments with interpersonal self-fulfilling prophecies in a school system, *Pygmalion in the Classroom*.[1] In their book, Rosenthal and Jacobsen describe an elementary school where students are tested at the beginning of each year and then placed in a fast, medium, or slow activity grouping. The researchers picked the names of sixty-five students from the first to the sixth grades and told their teachers that they were intellectual "bloomers," meaning that on their own these students would demonstrate remarkable growth during the school year. The test scores of these children, in fact, did not indicate such growth possibilities. The students' names were actually chosen randomly from a file of those who had not distinguished themselves by their test scores.

The researchers found 1 year later that the average IQ of the students who had been identified as bloomers had increased almost four points more than had their classmates' average IQ. In the earlier grades the gains were even more dramatic with the bloomers' increases being more than twice the increases of their peers. The bloomers had indeed bloomed.

Rosenthal and Jacobsen conclude that it was not so much *what* the teachers said or did that communicated their high expectations as *how* they said and did things. By their facial expressions, postures, and touch, they communicated to the bloomers that they expected improved intellectual performance. In addition, the researchers indicate that the teachers watched their special children more closely, and this greater attentiveness led to rapid reinforcement of correct responses with a consequent increase in these pupils' learning and achievement. By their encouragement and support they undoubtedly had a favorable effect on the bloomers' motivation.

The bloomers were, no doubt, excited to have such attention, especially since it did not carry recrimination. They were able to try out new ideas, ask questions, and get help because they knew that they would receive a favorable response from someone whose role represented authority and achievement. Their confidence and self-respect were heightened because someone who was important to them considered their strivings worthwhile and their accomplishments, however small they might be, significant.

We are always building on models and heroes—people who are important to us. As we gain new experiences, we incorporate some of the values and perspectives of people who are close to us. We take a part of them and add it to ourselves. We particularly incorporate the expectations which we pick up from significant others toward us. That's why managers can exert such a powerful influence on others—those whom they supervise are probably modeling themselves on their bosses, learning from them, fulfilling their expectations, however subtly or unknowingly such expectations may be conveyed.

It is highly unlikely that employees will change substantially their basic personality structures or their pattern of psychological defenses, but they may change drastically their orientation toward people in various situations. Each of us learns to conduct ourselves somewhat differently for the different kinds of situations in which we are called on to perform and for the different kinds of roles we are expected to take. Thus, we are somewhat different at work than at home, and we present ourselves somewhat differently to our spouse than to our boss, to our peers than to our children, to our doctor than to a door-to-door sales representative, and so on. Almost intuitively, we size up a situation, size up what is expected of us in that situation, and act accordingly.

In the continued presence of someone we respect, moreover, we can not only take on but also learn to act out new images of ourselves. We can acquire new attitudes and values, new competencies, and new ways of conducting ourselves in interpersonal situations through social interaction. The research evidence for this proposition that we pick up the attitudes and incorporate the values of people who are important to us is quite impressive. The evidence suggests that people do what people who are personally important to them think they should do.

Everyday Life

On a Wednesday morning in 1932, Cartwright Millingville comes to work. His place of business is the Last National Bank, and the office he occupies is that of its president. The tellers' windows, he notes, are rather busy for a Wednesday. Long lines of depositors are unusual for midweek, so far from payday. Millingville hopes sympathetically that they have not been laid off, and he begins his presidential chores. The Last National Bank is a sound and solvent institution. Its president knows that, its stockholders know that, and we know that. But the people in those lines before the tellers' cages don't know that. They, in fact, believe that the bank is foundering, that if they do not quickly withdraw their deposits, there will be none to withdraw, and so they are lined up now, waiting to withdraw their savings. Until they believed that and acted on their belief, they were quite wrong. But once they believed it and acted upon it, they "knew" a truth or reality unknown to Cartwright Millingsville, unknown to the stockholders, and unknown to us. They knew that truth or reality because they caused that truth or reality. Their expectation, their prophecy, led to its own fulfillment. The bank failed.

It is not only the collapse of economic institutions that has been attributed to the operation of the self-fulfilling prophecy. Robert Morton of Columbia University, who first described the demise of Millingville's bank, also pointed out the importance of such expectations in the relations between races and the behavior of minority groups generally. Inferiority of scholastic achievement among blacks of a given state may indeed have become a reality when that state spent less than one-fifth as much in the education of its black youth as with its white youth.

Another major theorist to employ the concept of the self-fulfilling prophecy was Gordon Allport. His application was to the field of international tension and war. It was likely, Allport suggested, that nations that expect to go to war, go to war. The expectation to wage war is communicated to the opponent-to-be, who reacts by preparing for war, an act which confirms the first nation's expectation, strengthens it, leads to greater preparations for war, and so on, in a mutually reinforcing system of positive feedback loops. Nations expecting to remain out of wars sometimes seem to manage to avoid entering into them.

The effects on a person's behavior of the expectancies others have of that behavior is further illustrated by the learning theorist E. R. Guthrie. A shy and socially inept young woman became self-confident and relaxed in social contacts by having been systematically treated as a social favorite. A helpful group of college men had arranged the expectancies of those who met her so that socially adept behavior was expected of her. The expected adeptness was duly evoked by the expectation for it. In both civilian and military disasters, the victims seem to respond in accordance with the response expected of them by the rescue workers. Psychiatric experience in the U.S. Army seems to suggest that the more clearly a psychiatric casuality is treated as such, the less likely it is that the person can return to duty. In the more everyday experience of driving an automobile, it has been pointed out that one driver's expectation of another's automotive behavior can serve as self-fulfilling prophecy.

Hawthorne Effect

The Hawthorne effect derives its name from research done more than 50 years ago by two Harvard Business School professors, Fritz Roethlisberger and Elton Mayo, with the Hawthorne plant of the Western Electric Company. The researchers at Hawthorne began by studying the effects of such factors as lighting, heat, fatigue, and physical layout upon productivity. A group of workers was selected for the first experiment, which was aimed at identifying the effects of lighting upon output. It was found that as illumination was increased in the test group, production also increased. Furthermore, when the lighting intensity was decreased in the test group below the original levels, it was found that output still improved. It was not until the intensity of illumination had been decreased to the equivalent of ordinary moonlight that there was any appreciable decline in output.

The lighting study showed that positive results in productivity can be achieved independently of the content of changes which may be implemented. Thus, the Hawthorne effect is a term used to describe the results of an experimental effect or change program where positive results are related to employees feeling specially selected and believing in the wisdom of the experimenter or change agent. The Hawthorne effect also suggests that people who feel specially selected to show an effect will tend to show it.

Eaton Industries, headquartered in Cleveland, Ohio, has actively tried to use this idea to improve the quality of work life and the output of workers at its new factories. Plant management personnel indicate that what they are trying to do is to "bottle" the Hawthorne effect. This is done by allowing workers to be involved in making changes in their work routine and job layout. Since workers have an active voice in changes in equipment or personnel policies which affect them, they tend to be more committed to making those changes work. The results have been quite impressive when this approach has been taken at newer plant locations. Not only are absenteeism and turnover much lower at these plant locations than at other locations in the company, but start-up costs and output are also much better than they are at the more traditional plants.

David McClelland, a prominent management consultant, also believes that the Hawthorne effect can be bottled—especially in attempting to change business procedures or managerial practices. He maintains that the belief in the possibility and desirability of change is tremendously influential in changing a person. So he uses the authority of his own research findings, the suggestive power of membership in an experimental group, and his own personal prestige when working with managers to establish his personal base as an authority and utilize the power of the Hawthorne effect. His record of success would indicate that what he does certainly works. These examples serve to illustrate the basis of the Hawthorne effect and establish the validity of the concept of interpersonal self-fulfilling prophecy. These two concepts are essentially different terms for the same phenomenon. People tend to do or believe what is expected of them, especially when the person holding an expectation is a prestigious source.

Placebo Effect

Physicians have long recognized that their ability to inspire both trust and the patient's expectation of healing partially determines the success of treatment. At times, doctors have resorted to the use of a placebo, a pharmacologically inert substance such as a sugar pill or a water injection, to relieve a patient's distress. Studying the reactions of patients to placebos is another means of studying the effects of expectations on behavior.

Evidence that placebos can have marked physiological effects and even heal tissue damage is impressive. The placebo treatment of warts, for example, by painting them with a brightly colored dye and telling the patient that the wart will be gone by the time the color wears off, is as effective in wart removal as any other treatment, including surgical excision.

Placebo treatment can also activate healing of more severely damaged tissue. In an experimental study of patients hospitalized with bleeding peptic ulcers, 70 percent showed "excellent results lasting over a period of one year" when a doctor gave them an injection of distilled water and assured them that it was a new medicine that would cure them.

Placebos have also been shown to be effective in causing the remission of cancer, curing colds, and eliminating a variety of other maladies. Placebos produce an effect based solely on a patient's confidence in a physician. This resembles the "hello–good-bye" effect in psychotherapy. Studies have been conducted which show that patients with emotional distresses who merely have contact with a prestigeful medical authority improve almost as much as those who get prolonged therapy.

None of these reported results is intended to demonstrate that many people are hypochondriacs or that most ailments are simply "all in your head." Such a conclusion would be erroneous. Rather, these studies supply more evidence that our belief in another person's ability is an important element of that person's efficacy as a healing agent.

Summary

One person's expectations of another person's behavior strongly affect what that other person does. When we hold expectations regarding someone else, our expectations can subtly, but powerfully, serve as an interpersonal self-fulfilling prophecy. This fact can be observed and has been documented in a variety of settings. It is possible, moreover, for managers to create high performance expectations and get better results from those whom they supervise.

Such expectations depend on more than wishing and must be more than the power of positive thinking. Managers must realize that how they treat others communicates their expectations more convincingly than what they may say to them. Moreover, their ability to get results depends on their confidence in themselves, the confidence and self-esteem they build in others, and the confidence which others have in them.

Something is going on in the minds of effective managers which is foreign to their less effective counterparts. Effective managers seem to be more aware of who they are and what they want and consequently find it unnecessary to look to others for direction and guidance. They are not loners; they enjoy being with people and enjoy recognition, but the praise and status which others can bestow on effective managers serve to confirm the image managers already have of themselves. Since status and praise do not create this image, the image is not dependent on them.

The high expectations which effective managers have of others are simply an extension of the expectations which they have of themselves. What managers believe about themselves—their ability to perform required tasks well—powerfully influences what they believe about others and, in turn, what others believe about them. Managers who can learn to have confidence in themselves can learn to have confidence in others and to communicate their expectations in such a way that they will become self-fulfilling prophecies.

Someone who believes that gaining self-confidence is difficult will find that it is so. Self-fulfilling prophecies are most effective regarding what we think we can do. Yet, believing that we can be more self-confident is only the beginning. We must do something which demonstrates to ourselves that we are worthy, capable, and competent. Once we have a stockpile of accomplishments and a baseline of self-regard, the recognition of others can sustain us and encourage us to do better and better.

References

1. Rosenthal, Robert, and Lenore Jacobsen: *Pygmalion in the Classroom* (New York: Holt, Rinehart and Winston, 1968).

Chapter 5

Counseling Employees: Developing Problem-Solving Skills and Enhancing Competence

Jane was concerned. She closed her office door behind her and sat at her desk mulling over the situation. Ever since she had assumed responsibility for the department 4 months ago, she had worked hard to turn things around, to improve the sagging performance of a staff group who had seemed to grow tired and weary—discouraged, in fact, because their advice was seldom sought or their recommendations adopted. Now she was pondering what to do about Ray.

Ray was the senior employee in the department. At 52, he was more than 20 years older than anyone else in the group. Well-liked and easygoing, Ray had been expected by most of the others in the group to be the next department head. Ray had shared their expectations. He was visibly disappointed, while others were silently resentful, when a new person—a stranger—was brought in to supervise the group. "Ray sure got the shaft," some said.

Jane had worked hard to win the respect of the group. She could be tough when she had to make an important decision. Decisive, that was it. And aggressive and thorough. Jane was technically well-suited to manage the department, and others quickly saw that. But in 4 months she had been unable to eliminate Ed's rumored backbiting and resentment toward her or erase Ray's disappointment even though Ray said little about it.

Now Jane was considering what she should do about it. Ray didn't have the ability of others who were vying for promotions to department head, and such positions didn't open up very often either. Should she "lay it on the line" with Ray or "lead him along—hold out the promise of a promotion in order to solicit his cooperation? Or should she try to get Ray a new title or some other symbol of status that might ease his personal sense of loss even though there would be no substance to the change? And what about Ed? He was technically very capable, but was making careless mistakes. If Jane confronted him, would it simply increase Ed's bitterness? Jane had only some hints about Ed's spreading of rumors—should she confront that activity too or hope that things would work out with time? Jane did not want to create problems that were not there, but she also wanted to act quickly and "nip in the bud" any potential problems. That's why she sat concerned in her office with her door closed. She didn't know what to do—and that was unusual for her.

Almost every manager faces similar situations on an everyday basis. Since "management" is "getting things done through people," managers face the sometimes awesome task of finding the right incentives, providing the right challenge, and giving the right recognition to the people they direct. Managers, however, must also be adept at binding up bruised egos, salving hurt feelings, and reducing pressures and tensions if they are to be as effective as possible. But too many managers find themselves in an uncomfortable position when they are required to confront, correct, coach, or counsel those who report to them. The same manager who can comfortably make a multimillion dollar investment decision and feel little stress in the process may go to great lengths to avoid the uncomfortable feeling of dealing face-to-face with those who are embittered or less capable.

These and other problem employees can be found in almost every office. And each office develops its own dynamics to deal with them. Unfortunately, the means developed are often neither direct nor personal. Elaborate conspiracies can grow up in some offices so that co-workers avoid those who don't perform or humor into impotence (under the guise of kindness) those who can't perform.

The fundamental truth in the scenario just presented is the difficulty in dealing with emotions and feelings—the human problems of people at work. It is much easier to emphasize "honesty" and "openness" in work organizations than it is to achieve them. Such ideals, even when accepted, produce dilemmas even for those well-skilled in interpersonal relations. It is not easy to deal with the human problems of people at work, but it is important. One recent survey cited the need for counseling with people effectively in a one-to-one relationship as the single most important need in management development today.

Every manager needs to be able to handle the difficult human situations that can require understanding as well as negotiation. Managers have work needs and expectations to be met. Resolving "people problems" does not imply that managers simply "give in." In many situations, what may initially sound to a noninvolved listener like a case of an unsympathetic boss upon further investigation may prove instead to be a case of an unreasonable employee. The crucial questions in such situations are *not* who is to blame but *how* can things be improved. Since managers are in an authority position and usually charged with the responsibility to achieve their own units' work goals, upon them falls the burden of initiating action. So, to them falls the challenge of re-energizing a discouraged employee or recycling a bored worker or redirecting someone who is not performing up to standard.

Counseling—A Perspective

Counseling is an effective means of increasing the confidence and completeness of people and thereby building their self-esteem. Since management is essentially utilizing the abilities and capacities of people to get things done, it also seems apparent that managers must develop the potential of employees if they are to utilize them effectively.

One study of the effectiveness of counseling has been reported by Walter Mahler and William Wrightnour. They studied the practices of 210 managers in three different organizations: a manufacturing company, a supermarket chain, and a public utility. The results suggest that when managers and others spend a portion of their time counseling employees either by formal, systematic interviews or by informal sessions, the employees:

1. Feel more satisfied with their work
2. Believe their managers supervise them adequately
3. Report that they like the way their bosses motivate them

Counseling can provide a service to both the organization and the individuals within it who have particular problems. Counseling can provide a release for the frustrations that are an inevitable part of human interaction in an organization. Since counseling provides a forum for expressing personal frustrations, it also provides the promise of defusing and managing them. The alternative to promoting and encouraging such counseling is described by Frederick Herzberg:

> Implicit in the psychological contract between a manager and his subordinates is the clause, "If you work for me, I'm going to have to frustrate you sometimes." Any time you manage people you have to frustrate them—it's the name of the game and no amount of agonizing is going to negate this reality. However, the danger to the organization lies in extending this tacit contract to include the statement, "When I do frustrate you don't you dare express your hostility to me—I am the boss. Go home and kick your dog or go eat your heart out—that is, turn the hostility back on yourself."[1]

A work situation where frustrations arise and opportunities for expressing and dissipating concerns are not provided experiences both high personal and high organizational costs.

Counseling can also increase employee identification with the organization that employs them. It can reduce the feelings of estrangement that are especially prevalent in many large organizations. The fact is that there are typically only feeble attempts at mutual employer-employee problem solving in most organizations. Few attempts are made to reorganize discouraged people or recycle bored workers. So conflicts exist in an uneasy détente, frustrations continue unchecked, and unconscious conspiracies develop that suggest "Don't get too close; I don't want to get too involved." Knowing how and when to utilize appropriate counseling skills can counter such trends. With knowledge and skills, the manager or trainer need not shy away from dealing with emotions—anger or tears or resentment. One's own fears about competence can thus be dealt with more easily.

The changing nature of today's work force, a phenomenon that has been extensively documented, provides another reason to integrate counseling into organizational practices. Sunshine laws and privacy legislation reflect the desires of workers who want to know the what and why of policies that affect them. They want to have a dialogue on matters that were once left to management discretion. Personnel policies and practices are on the verge of becoming transparent.

People do not always know what they want or the costs associated with getting it. Yet, although they may be unclear about their goals and values, they may still have a vague sense that they are not keeping up with everyone else. We all know that we do not want to be left out or left behind when it comes to getting the rewards available through the organization that employs us. We want to be considered normal, of course, to be accepted, but we do not want to be considered average. In fact, one survey of employees in a large multinational company revealed that nearly 80 percent of the employees considered themselves to be among the top performers in the company. Reconciling aspirations with organizational options, managing disappointment, clarifying values, specifying goals—all these demands and others require that the effective counselor perform a variety of different roles. Doing this while keeping employees continuously engaged and productive is all part of the balancing act and synthesizing role of the counselor.

Counseling is a means to resolve conflicts, overcome resistance to change, utilize information, plan careers, make decisions, and give advice. Yes—give advice. Some problems will never be solved unless advice is given. Listening, paraphrasing, and seeking to understand another's point of view are necessary in all counseling situations, but alone are not sufficient in many of them. Giving advice, providing direction, or explaining a personal perspective is important if counseling discussions are actually going to resolve the problem at hand.

When managers counsel employees, it is important that they listen in order to understand. Knowing when someone just wants a "sounding board" needs to be discerned. But this is not enough in many employee counseling situations. Why? Because the reasons people seek out (or need) counseling in a work situation are often different from the reasons someone meets with a mental health counselor. In some cases, employees are troubled and can develop solutions to their own problems through a nondirective approach. In other cases, however, the basis of an employee problem is not an internal emotional conflict, but the result of frustration with company policy, uncertainty over role requirements, or insecurity about skills and abilities. In such cases, the information and advice (the counsel) sought or needed could not be developed by the employee through continuously having his or her thoughts and feelings paraphrased and restated. As the old adage goes, "You can't draw water from an empty well." Good information, including the experience of others in similar situations, is needed.

Good information is a scarce resource in many organizations. Although computers have enabled managers to collect tremendous quantities of data and even experience "information overload," information on how things "really" work remains difficult to retrieve and disseminate. Whether the labels describe the informal system or the politics of the organization, the fact remains that few people in most organizations have the information they need to plan their careers effectively, develop their skills and abilities fully, and match their interests with organizational goals appropriately. When this information isn't appropriately relayed in counseling discussions, both the individual and the organization suffer. Besides being seen in dissatisfaction and lethargy on the job, the effects of such informational failures also can be manifest in increased turnover and reduced productivity.

A manager as counselor develops an appropriate counseling perspective in addition to learning counseling skills. This counseling perspective suggests a focus on resolving individual problems and not on overhauling employees' personalities. At the workplace, the role of the counselor is more akin to an eye specialist than a painter: instead of creating a scene that represents reality, he or she widens and broadens perspectives so that reality can be seen more clearly.

It is imperative that the person doing counseling, as in the case of doctors and lawyers, be respected and well-regarded by those who receive his or her advice. Although the importance of trust and credibility is often stressed, there is little written material available on how these qualities can be demonstrated to those being counseled. Sidney Jourard provides a notable exception to this trend. At one point in his book, *The Transparent Self,* he describes how one can develop openness and cultivate confidence during a counseling discussion. Jourard says that he does things quite differently now from what he did when he first began in the counseling field.

> I reflect feelings and content as I always did but only when I want the [other person] to know that I really heard what he had to say. But now I find myself sometimes giving advice, lecturing, becoming angry, interrupting. . . .[2]

Jourard's point is that no one is interested in being counseled by someone who hides behind a sterile mask of objectivity. Who, after all, wants to be treated as an object? We want to interact with others who can show their humanity and demonstrate that they understand our problems. We are relieved when people we regard show their humanity. We are more likely to drop our defenses and openly explore options to a problem when we are not constrained by objectivity. Jourard is suggesting that a person wanting to do counseling unfortunately only gets invited to a discussion of the real problem when he or she gets subjectively involved. The counselor may free the other person up to explore options that may require the alteration of a typical habit pattern.

The issue surrounding subjectivity is not whether, but when. How does a person doing counseling know when to give advice and when to listen? How can one tell when advising will be interpreted as browbeating instead of path defining? Who can be sure that getting angry won't further complicate an already tense situation? Besides having clear answers to questions such as these, a counselor must be able to resolve such dilemmas as being able to:

- Give advice without creating dependency
- Contribute to the development of options without being parental and forcing strictly personal views on another
- Point to the likely consequences of various courses of action without being condescending
- Assist in decision making without being superficial

These are important and cannot be resolved easily or abstractly; much of what is appropriate depends on the situation.

At this point, my purpose is simply to point to some of the possible pitfalls and dilemmas encountered in counseling. It is not sufficient that someone wants to be an effective counselor. It is necessary to know how to be effective in a way that comes across as being effective.

Counseling Skills

Counseling is partially an art, partially a science. There are some basic procedures and principles that are important in effective counseling, but underlying these procedures is a basic orientation that suggests people can change and develop through mutual interaction. Counseling implies a general orientation and set of skills focused on assisting people in increasing their competence and increasing their control over their world. It is action-oriented and goal-oriented and recognizes the constraints and contexts of work organizations. Counseling is a general term which can and will be described in three different contexts: correcting, coaching, and consulting.

Correcting people who have specific performance problems is a necessary function of counseling. In any organization, there are formal work rules and informal group norms that keep the group or the organization functioning at a productive level. Both work rules and group norms can be dysfunctional and counterproductive. But likewise, any organization needs both these formal and these informal ways of doing things in order to function on a daily basis. Those who violate the more formal work rules must be confronted and dealt with appropriately if group efficiency is to be maintained.

Perhaps no one has illustrated the negative effects that result from a manager's allowing continued violation of work group rules as much as David McClelland of Harvard has. Professor McClelland has written an intriguing article entitled "Good Guys Make Bum Bosses." The basis of the article revolves around those who try simply to please subordinates and not enforce work rules and who are inevitably going to be accused of favoritism. In their efforts to please everyone, they will please no one. Rules and standards provide a sense of security for people in the work force. They demonstrate a concern of supervisors for the welfare of everyone. When they are followed, cooperation results. When any employees are allowed to indiscriminately violate work rules, chaos results.

Coaching is another counseling process. This aspect keys on performance discrepancies. If people know what to do but are not performing adequately, a coaching interview may be needed. The basic notion of coaching is that someone else observing our action is usually more aware of things we do than we are. Like an athletic coach, a person doing coaching in an organization is skilled in observation and in describing how employees can improve performance and then assisting them in doing so.

The third aspect of counseling is that of consulting or one-to-one problem solving. When people have concerns which derive from their work group environment, or their home environment, consulting may be needed. Unless they are adequately dealt with, concerns developed either at work or at home can spill over into other aspects of the person's life. Most of us from time to time enjoy and appreciate simply discussing our worries, anxieties, disappointments, and fears with others. If we know that we can get an empathetic ear and perhaps some good information, we are much more eager to share those often hidden concerns we carry with us. The intent of consulting is to enable a person to define more accurately a problem he or she has encountered, identify a course of action, anticipate possible unintended negative consequences from this course of action, and plan a specific personal strategy to improve the situation.

Correcting

The prime function of this type of counseling is not to determine an appropriate punishment for poor performance, but to administer correction principles in such a way that it will prevent the particular person from breaking the work rule or failing to perform as expected in the future. The effectiveness of discipline really has nothing to do with the severity of the punishment. If anything, the ratio is inverse. The intent of correction—helping someone improve—then, must be paramount as a guiding principle in reviewing effective correction techniques. How can a supervisor or a personnel specialist correct the performance or behavior of others in a way that motivates rather than discourages and is positive rather than negative?

Most people in an organization tend to obey most of the rules most of the time. Supervisors' and personnel specialists' roles would be impossible if employees didn't. They would have to spend most of their time and energy identifying, processing, and evaluating infractions if people did not obey most of the work rules. On the other hand, there is something very real in the fact that many people like to flirt with taboos. D. H. Lawrence, in fact, quipped that "Mankind invented sin in order to enjoy the feeling of being naughty." Rule breaking perhaps affords analogous attractions. People are titillated by the thought of breaking a rule and getting away with it. All rule-breaking behavior may not fall into this category, but it is certainly true that many people break rules in order to establish the limit. They want to know just how far a manager or personnel specialist will go before defining a firm standard.

One possible way of dealing with the problem of how to achieve positive discipline is to determine the conditions under which an employee feels the least resentful toward correction. Douglas McGregor formulated what he called the "hot stove rule" as a basis for identifying conditions that promote positive discipline. McGregor said effective discipline was analogous to touching a hot stove. When you touch the stove, you know that you have done something wrong; the consequences are immediate, impersonal, predictable, and consistent. The hot stove rule comprises each of these characteristics. To extend the analogy, a person touching a hot stove knows immediately that the stove is hot. The outcome every time a person touches the stove is predictable. A hot stove will not burn a person some of the time and leave that person unburned at other times. It will be impersonal; that is, the stove will not burn one person, but not another. It will be consistent. Every time a hot stove is touched, the person will be burned.

Effective discipline incorporates the same principles. Correction needs to be *immediate*. Many problems can be nipped in the bud if they are dealt with at an early point. Talking about a problem as soon as a supervisor or personnel representative becomes aware of it can be the key to fairness and the sense of security that people desire at work. Adherence to work rules should be seen as similar to natural laws; that is, there are *predictable* consequences of following the rules and of not following the rules. People will feel better about following them and be more likely to obey them if consequences are certain. The third aspect of the hot stove rule is to be *impersonal*. When a manager is impersonal and focusing on the act, not the person, initial resentment is more likely to be minimized. In fact, a person who gets upset when disciplined will likely feel the same sheepishness as the cook who kicked the stove when she burned her hand. The final aspect of correction is *consistency*. The greater the inconsistency in administering work rules, the fiercer the resentment for the discipline. Individuals resent being singled out.

Correction that is immediate, predictable, impersonal, and consistent is more likely to achieve its intended aims than is correction that lacks these characteristics. Other important aspects of this type of counseling are the recognition that unless people know where they want to go, have a clear picture of the ideal target, as well as a clear idea of the first step, and have some particular incentive for changing, correction is not likely to produce the desired result. Simply, one needs a direction, a starting point, and a destination. A clear picture of the ideal target is necessary in order for a person to know that the future outcome is going to be worth the journey. A clear view of the ideal target impels a person to desire the change. Likewise, a clear perception of the first step enables a person to go from the abstract to the specific with knowledge of what and when. An incentive to change is another key element. Without an incentive to perform differently, a desired destination and a road map won't get a person off dead center. Creating a discrepancy between where a person is and where that person wants to be is a very effective technique in providing an incentive to change. Hope or optimism is an alternative to the discrepancy technique for enabling a person to change; conveying an optimistic sense of "you can do it" can be a tremendous fuel for a person whose energy seems to be limited.

To see the application of these ideas, let's look at an ordinary situation:

I Was Only a Few Minutes Late

SITUATION

Phil Sanders is a recently hired employee. He is assigned as a clerical assistant, and this is his first real job other than occasional day labor. He is 18, and dropped out of high school 2 years ago, but has recently been going to night school to get a high school certificate. When Dottie Moffet, the supervisor, hired him, she knew that she would need to work carefully with Phil to explain the job, answer questions, and generally be a resource to him. His first day on the job, Dottie spent a lot of time with Phil and felt that she had made progress in working with him. All was well for the first few days until Phil came into work about an hour late.

Dottie: Phil, I'd like to talk with you for a few minutes if I could.

Phil: Sure, Dottie. What's on your mind?

Dottie: I am really pleased to have you working for us, Phil. I feel like the first few days you made a good impression on several people and tried hard to hold your job.

Phil: Well thanks, Dottie. Uh, what else is on your mind, though?

Dottie: I think you had a really good beginning coming in 4 days in a row on time. Today was really your first miss. Phil, it is important for everyone to come to work on time. We all depend on one another.

Phil: I know that, Dottie; I don't want to let anybody down. Actually, I intended to come to work on time, but I had car trouble.

Dottie: I know things come up from time to time. If you know you are going to be late for some reason, though, it is important to call your supervisor. You knew that, didn't you?

Phil: Yes, I guess I did. I just forgot to call. I thought it would be easier if I worked on the car and came in as soon as I could.

Dottie: I am glad that you are here and that you came in as soon as you could. But I do want to stress the importance of calling if you're going to be late or not going to be here at all. I also think it is important to come to work on time everyday. And as I say, things do come up, but we do expect everybody to be at work on time everyday, unless there is some extenuating circumstance.

Phil: I know that, and I will be at work on time from now on.

Dottie: I know you will be able to do it, too, Phil, if you work on it. Sometimes it's not easy to get up in the morning and plan a day. Especially when the night before you may have had other things to do and couldn't check on things, or maybe unexpected things come up, like car trouble. But I think it is important to realize that we all have a responsibility to be at work as well.

Phil: I know that, Dottie, and I don't think this is anything to get upset about. It only happened once. You said it is only the first day I've missed.

Dottie: I know it is something that only happened once, and I am really glad for the days that you have come to work on time. I just want you to know that tardiness and absenteeism are things we all need to control. There are procedures that management estab-lished as work rules for all of us, so that we all feel like we have the same standards. Probably the thing that can reduce morale in a work group quicker than anything is if the boss is seen by employees as giving one person preferential treatment. I want you to know, Phil, that every time you're late or absent, I want to talk with you about it. That doesn't mean that I don't trust you, or that I think you've done anything wrong, except that I want to treat you the same as every other employee. Any time any other employee in the plant is late on my shift, I talk to them; likewise, any time an employee is absent, I want everybody to know that we have no part-time jobs and also that we are all expected to live up to the same standards. I think it is important to treat everybody the same, don't you, Phil?

Phil: Yes, I do. I'm glad that you are willing to treat me the same as everyone else, and I'm going to do better.

Dottie: That's great. I'm glad. I really am glad to have you as an em-ployee, Phil, and I think you are going to make a good contribu-tion. I'm also glad for our little talk. And please remember to call if you're going to be late or absent for any reason. Establish this precedent, that regardless of the reason for lateness or absentee-ism, I'm going to have a little talk with you and with anyone else.

I am concerned for your well-being as well as with establishing fairness and uniformity by treating you the same as others. Thanks for the chat. See you later, Phil.

Dottie: Thanks for talking, Dottie. See you later.

CRITIQUE

Dottie either has learned or knows intuitively about reinforcement and control. It is especially important in dealing with an employee who is new or feels a little insecure to place stress on positive aspects of performance. Discipline or expressed reprisal is likely to have negative effects, produce temper outbursts, or create a desire to get back at the boss in some other way, possibly, even through resignation.

A supervisor who patiently encourages an employee and reminds the person about what still remains to be done to meet the total job requirements will most effectively handle problems such as this. It is just as important to be firm on standards as it is to show concern. This takes conscious effort on the part of the supervisor to avoid a more obvious emotional reaction or temptation such as: "He let me down; he's just as I thought he would be—inadequate. The only thing he will ever understand is discipline. I'll show him who's boss here." Such attitudes and perspectives are likely to produce negative rather than positive results. Someone who has never been required to be on time, who has never had the importance of being on time stressed, who feels that excuses can be offered and absenteeism or lateness justified will continue to be late and develop or make up reasons for being so. It is natural to expect that a person who is absent or late has a devious excuse and will be both on the offensive and embarrassed when approached. Calling employees on the carpet, questioning their integrity, will not produce desired results. The liklihood is that it will only make them angry. It is important in such cases to be supportive and positive and to know things employees have done well in order to build the necessary self-confidence—the feelings of acceptance in the employees. Similarly, it is necessary to let employees know that rules or standards must be abided by.

The supervisor, in this vignette, not only was positive in encouraging the employee by noting things he had done well during the first few days of work, but also was positive in stressing the importance of being on time and the fact that a supervisory discussion could be expected every time someone came in late or returned from an absence. The reason for the lateness or the absenteeism did not matter—the fact that it occured was justification for the discussion. The mere fact of having a discussion, of stressing the importance of standards, not acknowledging the validity of whatever reason for absenteeism was given, will serve as an effective reinforcement tool which will let the employee have an opportunity to produce positive results at work. Proper reinforcement requires frequent contact and feedback and prompt response on the part of the supervisor. Unfortunately, it takes time on the supervisor's part. The problem will not go away by itself. It needs to be confronted and dealt with in a positive rather than punitive manner. A supervisor needs to be matter-of-fact rather than vindictive about enforcing rules. If enforcement of rules is consistent and uniform, that is, if truly no one is treated differently, it is rare that the discipline will be resented. Obviously, and with individual differences, the manager must expect to devote extra time and effort if he or she is genuinely interested in improving in these matters.

Coaching

Perhaps there is no more traditional function that is seen as an integral part of management than coaching. It is almost accepted as a given that managers should help those whom they supervise to achieve desired performance standards. Coaching differs from correcting in a subtle but important manner. In correcting, a manager emphasizes a specific standard of performance or teaches a basic skill. In coaching, a manager is aiming at improved performance or increased competence in an employee. Correcting focuses on prior behavior, while coaching focuses on future performance. Coaching attempts to build competence or enhance motivation, while correcting describes specific performance deficiencies. Coaching focuses on *improved* performance instead of *non*performance, emphasizing that more or better results could be achieved although current activities are not acceptable.

Many managers find it useful to employ specific and quantitative performance measures as the basis for improving results. Energy and enthusiasm are released by having reasonable goals and striving to achieve them.

But it is likewise important in coaching to be a little wary of these potent tools and notice the possible unintended negative consequences that they include. Here are some examples:

1. The telephone company began measuring the performance of wirers who handle changes in telephone numbers. They did this by counting the number of new connections wirers made each day. The wirers, aware of increased emphasis on this particular standard of performance, began neglecting to remove excess wires associated with disconnected numbers, and the panels grew overweight with excessive waste wire. Some even collapsed. Because removing un-

necessary wire was not specifically measured and went unnoticed, the procedure became neglected.

2. A computer company began measuring the performance of computer repairers by the speed with which they accomplished specific repairs in a customer's home. To look good on more difficult repairs, the repairers ignored early reports from customers on diagnostically difficult problems and waited until the problem worsened or was repeated. The customers were incensed by this increase in downtime. The repairers, on the other hand, were rewarded for the speed with which they were able to diagnose these difficult problems.

3. School teachers in a local school district, whose competency was measured on the basis of student's examination results, began to teach the tests and ignore other classroom activities. Priming sessions were conducted in advance on national tests, and, rather than being reinforced in the basics, students for several months of the year simply learned how to pass this particular test.

The total organization may be the loser when motivation targets are overly stressed or misused. Unmeasured aspects of the job may then be ignored, and larger organizational interests may be disregarded. Often, cooperation between groups becomes a thing of the past. Subordinates, single-mindedly pursuing a goal of increased performance, are in no mood to consider the needs of adjacent work groups for better quality, change in schedule, or any other accommodation for that matter, when only performance is emphasized. There must be a balance between overall standards of performance and other aspects of the work that are important and necessary and that contribute to the overall performance of a work group or an organization.

A specific approach to employee motivation that has been recently identified and regularly used is called the path-goal theory. This theory reverses the long-standing assumption of most managers that satisfied employees will be more productive. Instead, the notion maintains that employees must perceive productivity and performance as necessary steps along their paths to satisfying their own goals. That is, improved performance is something that is related to the employee's own self-interest. There are many links in the chain for the path-goal theory to work—for employees to be motivated.

The leaders, managers, and personnel specialists must do much more than offer reward for a job well-done. The link of the extended chain must be satisfied. The following basic elements seem to be necessary for the path-goal conditions to be met:

1. Employees must have the capacity, through past experiences and their self-confidence, to improve their own performance.

2. This improved performance will not be excessively costly in terms of devoting individual energy, disrupting friendships, or making other personal sacrifices.
3. This improved performance will result in demonstratively good results, that is, something that others can measure, assess or perceive, some significant difference from the situation before. Again, the results may be in the areas of energy, friendship, or other personal satisfaction.
4. The results will be rewarded, and the reward will be perceived as equitable by the subordinate in this particular matter.

Subordinates obviously have their own interests, often different from those of the manager, and they have their own views of situations, as well. Either their interests, or their views, or both, may cause them to sidestep their responsibilities or to participate in goldbricking on the job. Such nonperformance can embarrass and handicap managers seeking credibility and support. How do they confront the reluctant subordinate? The "no" may take the form of a subtle refusal to accept a change in methods, a new procedure or activity; or a refusal to finish an assignment in the face of an obstacle; or a reluctance to redo an unacceptable assignment. There may be a hundred other possibilities in which the manager's perceptions of what is needed differ from the subordinate's view of what is equitable or desirable or necessary. And in most organizations there will always be good and sufficient reasons why something can't be done: lack of time or resources, another department's failure to fulfill a commitment, contrary policy, conflicting rules, and the like. Whatever the source, and whether it's due to simple recalcitrance, misunderstanding, or a desire to challenge the boss, it can become a crucial test of the manager's coaching skills.

Let's look at another ordinary situation and see how coaching skills can be developed and used.

There's So Much Stress in This Job

SITUATION

Harold Bronson was recently promoted to supervising engineer responsible for about ten design engineers and drafters. He has seemed to have experienced some difficulty in making the transition from an individual contributor to a supervisor. In particular, he has been rather moody and irritable lately—quite a contrast from the almost happy-go-lucky fellow who was promoted 3 months ago. His boss, Lynn Reece has decided to talk to him about it, and after some casual conversation Harold brings up the topic himself.

Harold: You know, Lynn, I just can't seem to get my act together and do this job well. There just seems to be so much stress in this job, so much pressure for me to perform, so many demands. I really have a hard time thinking.

Lynn: What kind of demands do you feel, Harold?

Harold: Oh, demands from everybody. Demands on my time from subordinates, pressure to perform and complete projects so as to meet all deadlines, and pressure to perform well socially. We've recently been invited to several social events that people in the company have sponsored. I even feel pressure to perform there. I take work home every night; I never seem to have enough time to take a vacation day, just take a day off, or even go out for a relaxing lunch. I feel uptight, nervous, and tense a lot. I don't know, I just don't seem to be coping with it all very well.

Lynn: It seems that at least you have identified that you have a problem in this area.

Harold: Yeah, I've got a problem, all right. I've got lots of problems. My problem is not that it's difficult to see; my problem is what to do about it.

Lynn: I think I hear you saying, Harold, that you feel fairly confident that the problem you have is the stress in your life: the demands, the pressures, and the difficulty of coping with them.

Harold: That's right. What do I do to cope with such stress?

Lynn: Well, I think one of the most popular solutions is to meditate and spend some time relaxing and thinking about something else. There are many courses available on meditation, and a lot of good books as well.

Harold: No, no, I don't want to do that. You know, meditation may be good for some other people, but it's not for me. It seems so hokey to me, something that is faddish, that only somebody who is radical would even consider.

Lynn: You'd be inclined not to try meditation because of other people who are using it?

Harold: That's right. I don't want to be stereotyped by someone else. I want to try something that will work, not something that is off the wall.

Lynn: A number of executives have found relaxation techniques like meditation effective, Harold. I know its been used by a number of companies and has even been encouraged by some presidents of major corporations.

Harold: Well, it may work in other companies, but it wouldn't work here. No, Lynn, that isn't something for me. I think that would create more stress rather than reduce it. I'd feel I was doing something crazy, something that was not completely acceptable.

Lynn: Another approach that a number of individuals and companies as well have found useful is regular exercise each day. What would you think about working out in a gym or going jogging on a regular basis? What appeal does a planned exercise program have for you?

Harold: No, I don't think that will work for me, either. I know it will work for some people, Lynn, but I have tried exercise before. As a matter of fact, I get a lot of exercise. I walk to the bus stop and walk home, and I get some good exercise that way. You know, I think exercise is fine for the right people, but I do a lot of exercises and that doesn't seem to have helped me much. It doesn't seem to release any pressure. Most of the time when I go out and play golf or tennis, I feel even more competitive. It induces more pressure and creates more stress, rather than relieving it. No, I don't think that would work either. Besides, I don't have the time to do something that would take more time.

Lynn: Well, I guess another thing that people have tried and found to be useful is to identify stress indicators, things that tend to induce stress in you. For example, you say that sports create more stress rather than relieve it. Are there other job-related actions that create stress? Can you identify those conditions, those factors, and then when you see them on the horizon, use them as early-warning signals and realize that you may just need to talk to yourself, to say, "Hey, here's something I need to be calm about"? Maybe even try some breathing exercises. That has been a useful technique to reduce and cope with stress.

Harold: My problem is, Lynn, that everything right now causes and creates stress. Nothing seems to work in my favor, and everything I do seems to add more fuel to the fire. As for breathing exercises, I don't know, I don't see how that could be very effective.

Lynn: Well, what things have you considered trying?

Harold: Nothing, really, I just don't know what to do. If I knew what to do, I'd do it.

Lynn: What if I told you that we won the Ferguson contract and I was going to assign it to your group without reducing your workload?

Harold: Wow, the Ferguson project! What a challenge! But I'd go crazy, Lynn. Things wouldn't get done. I'd be a nervous wreck. You wouldn't do that to me, would you?

Lynn: If you had to do it all, how would you do some of the things differently than you're doing now?

Harold: Gee, I haven't even considered that possibility. I thought I was going to get less work or some good advice, not more wood added to the fire.

Lynn: What would you do?

Harold: If I didn't quit first, I suppose I'd assign Stevens to do the Benson project and try to consolidate the administrative work in Lee's area and talk to the group about other ways we could make ourselves more efficient. But we couldn't get everything done, Lynn, you'd just have to accept that. Some things would have to get shoved aside for a while. We'd have to really prioritize things and agree that we would do the most important things first and let some other things slide.

Lynn: Harold, we haven't gotten the Ferguson contract yet, but I think we should start right now in implementing some of these ideas you just came up with. They are the best things yet either one of us has said that can really help with reducing some of the stress you feel in your job.

Harold: You're right. I just never thought much about them although they aren't all that dramatically original. I guess I just never considered them until you made me consider how I would handle a "disaster situation." (laughing) Even though this has helped me, Lynn, if you did just add on the Ferguson situation, it would be a disaster.

COUNSELING

Much of this vignette presents a typical problem faced by counselors. They want to help, and they have some ideas which could be useful to the person they are counseling. But that other person isn't listening. For every suggestion the counselor offers, the employee has a reason why it can't work. This is an interpersonal game known as "Why don't you . . ."; "Yes, but . . ." because it follows a pattern of counselor hints and employee excuses. People who are avoiding some personal decision and looking for ways to avoid taking responsibility often play this game. Whatever the decision is they are avoiding, they are also trying to reduce their anxiety caused by not making a decision. They want to put the blame for things as they are on someone or something else and thus fill their time with discussions centered on the premise that they are not guilty of doing nothing themselves.

This particular interpersonal game is perhaps the most deceptive, and consequently the most common one, in which counselors participate.

They want to help, and so their good intentions get in the way of being helpful. When a counselor realizes that a counseling opportunity has turned into a "Why don't you . . ."; "Yes, but . . ." game, the following questions might be asked of the other person to generate a more productive mode:

- What do you think you should do?
- What have you already considered doing but rejected?
- What were the pluses and minuses of these options as you saw them?
- I feel as if you came here looking for advice or assistance, but you don't think what I have to say is very helpful. Is there something I can do to be more helpful?

Each of these questions will cause the person to reflect on the discussion and look at the problem from a more personal point of view.

When Lynn asked Harold what he would do if given the Ferguson project with no changes in his workload, she was using a powerful counseling technique. She gave Harold an "unexpected response." Harold was looking for ideas and assistance from Lynn but—without saying it—he was also seeking reassurance and consolation. Harold didn't really want to change his behavior and was merely seeking to justify his actions—to show why neither delegation nor personal coping skills would work in this situation. Lynn listened to this rationalization patiently for a time then asked Harold to consider an impossible situation. Its mere implausibility caused Harold to abandon his excuses and realize that he would have to rearrange his work and accept the reality that some things would—of necessity—go undone.

Giving an unexpected response can produce powerful results. Oftentimes managers are viewed as insincere in counseling because they offer clichés for advice which employees regard as the "same old company line." Or they are seen as divorced from reality—she doesn't understand my problems, she gives the same glib responses to any situation that I have." Giving unexpected responses shows that a manager doing counseling is sincere, and it breaks down the defensiveness that employees sometimes feel when being counseled. Unexpected responses also force people to consider new and different situations and overcome a tendency to resist change. They "unfreeze" thinking, get people who are "stuck" going again. There is a marriage counselor who asks couples who are having difficulties when they first come to him, "Why haven't you gotten a divorce yet?" He says most couples do not expect such a question from a marriage counselor and respond by saying, "I thought marriage counselors were supposed to save marriages, not encourage divorce." He insists on an answer, however, and finds that by his asking this unexpected question, couples stop personal cycles of blaming and are psychologically freed to consider what is truly important in their marriage.

It is easy for a counselor to get entwined in a "Why don't you . . ."; "Yes, but . . ." game with an employee who feels too much stress in his or her job. There are so many clichés and so many apparent solutions that work that a counselor may slip into this mode without even realizing it. This is because the human tendency is to be overwhelmed by tension and stress, and a counselor may try too hard to give the person techniques to resist it. An effective way of dealing with stress is to avoid what one observer calls "terrible simplifications." Too often we attempt to reduce a situation down to an either/or dilemma and then get cold feet about it. Common simplifications may be ones such as a choice for a man to "please my wife or please myself" in deciding on a promotion that would involve a relocation or a choice to "stand up for my rights" versus "turn the other cheek" in deciding how to respond to a racial or sexist joke. Tension increases with the importance of what we perceive as "no win" dilemmas.

Such stress-related concerns can often be reduced by making the dilemmas into objectives. How can I please my wife and myself? What do we really want? What conditions would make this move attractive to her? What would I be able to do to enjoy my work if I turned the promotion down? Instead of simplifying things, making them more complex can help us see what we really want to do and why, and thereby open a tension relief valve.

Consulting

The process of giving advice and imparting information is much more complex than we initially realize. On the surface, it seems rather easy and straightforward to tell someone who asks for advice exactly what we think. However, someone's request for information may be anything *but* a request for information. This is well-illustrated by an example developed by S. I. Hayakawa: Suppose you have a flat tire along the roadside and a passerby notices your predicament and stops. The first thing that the motorist is likely to say to you is, "Got a flat?" Certainly this is not a request for information. The person knew you had a flat tire before stopping. The question is rather one of testing your receptivity to and need for help. It is a method of introduction and not a question that is intended to be taken literally.

Perhaps the most difficult aspect of consulting is attempting to determine exactly how much advice and information the other person may be seeking and how much reassurance or support for a preconceived idea that is waiting to be expressed is being sought. Many people want to "test the water" before they are willing to openly express a particular concern or reveal their predetermined solution to a particular problem.

Norman R. F. Maier of the University of Michigan has extensively studied the essential role that talking a problem out plays in most of our lives. When we have a chance to discuss a problem, opportunity, or disappointment, we not only feel better ourselves but are more likely to develop a better and more stable solution to the situation we face. There is more than catharsis in the consulting relationship. There are also the seeds of effective problem solving and decision making.

The distinguishing feature of consulting is that an employee has a problem or concern and begins seeking the assistance of someone else. The focus of both correcting and coaching is with the manager who wants some form of changed behavior. The locus of control as well as the nature of the dialogue differs significantly, although the general goal of each is problem solving to develop enough competence and stability to deal with particular problems.

The fundamental difficulty in consulting is in overcoming the imbalance that exists. A manager not only occupies a position of authority and prestige but also is placed in the position of someone who can be a help and resource. The person asking for help puts himself or herself "one down" with respect to the helper by admitting that a problem exists, and the helper is automatically "one up" by being forced into the position of presumed expert. Building an effective relationship requires restoring a sense of compromise and balance between the employee and the counselor.

Perhaps consulting aspects that are a part of the counseling process can be well-illustrated through a specific example.

I'm Not Sure I Can Handle Moving Again

SITUATION

Don walked slowly back to his office from his boss's office. He closed the door, propped his feet on his desk, rolled a pencil over and over in his hand, and studied the rain spots on his window. Finally, he picked up the phone and called Judd, a senior accountant in the company and a close friend. Judd had taken a special interest in Don when he first transferred into the home office, and Don had often confided in him about personal problems as well as work-related problems.

Don: Judd? Do you have some time right now to talk? I need your advice.

Judd: Sure, come on over.

Don: (After a few minutes Don arrived and closed the door behind him as he walked into Judd's office.) Well, they're about to do it to me again.

Judd: Who? What?

Don: The suckers are about to transfer me again. After only 19 months here, they're about to do it to me again. I can't believe it! I have told practically everyone that I wanted to stay here for a while, to establish some roots in the community, to give my wife a chance to know her neighbors. "Fine," they all said. "This job needs someone in it for a while," they said. "Besides, we could move you into another section in the building when you're ready for something else so you wouldn't need to move again," they said. I just can't believe they would do this to me again!

Judd: Another move, eh?

Don: Yes, and to Los Angeles of all places. I just can't believe our enlightened management. They talk about being sensitive to employee needs and then do something like this to me.

Judd: Well, Don, if you really feel that strongly about it, don't go. I've known people who've turned down transfers and lived to tell about it.

Don: Oh, I know that. But I know the way those guys think, too. They'll say I'm not loyal, not willing to make some personal sacrifices in order to advance myself professionally. Listen, if I thought I wasn't going anywhere in the company, I'd turn down this transfer in a minute without any qualms. But I've been given a lot of encouragement in the last few years by people up the line. Unless they're just leading me on, they think I could go somewhere in the company.

Judd: Like Los Angeles? (laughter)

Don: Yeah, I guess. Like Los Angeles. What would you do, Judd?

Judd: I'm not sure I even understand all your feelings about the situation yet, Don, let alone have enough information to give any advice. Tell me, what would your new job be?

Don: I'd be the accounting supervisor in the budget planning section for the regional office there in L.A.

Judd: Mmmm. That would be a nice promotion for you.

Don: I know that. And I know some of the people out there and think highly of them. But I don't know anything about budget planning. As you know, all my experience has been in financial analysis. I know that kind of work, and know I can do well in it. Budget planning is an unknown quantity.

Judd: Do you feel that you can do that kind of work? Is part of your concern branching out into a new area?

Don: Partly, though I think it would be a good experience for me. Sure, I've some apprehension about doing well in the job, but what upsets me the most about this whole damn thing is the arbitrariness of it. I've told everyone I could that I didn't want to move again for a while—I think five moves in 9 years with the company is enough. I didn't want to be placed in a position like this of being forced to choose between my personal preferences and professional advancement. The thing is, Judd, I don't want to be possessed by my job, but I don't want to be left behind while others advance either.

Judd: I can understand that. Have you talked to your wife about this yet?

Don: Not yet. I wanted to think about it for a while by myself first.

Judd: How do you think she would feel about the move?

Don: If I felt strongly about it, she would go. She has gotten used to the moving game maybe even more than I have. She cares about me and wants me to be happy in what I do. Likewise, I care about her and want what's best for her. I don't want her to feel guilty about encouraging me to remain here if we decided to stay. Until I'm less confused about what I want, though, I don't think we can discuss the situation very well.

Judd: I agree that you need to decide what you want, but I think talking it out with your wife and others is the best way to decide. Most of us think better when we do it out loud.

Don: Okay. So where do I begin?

Judd: First of all, I think you need to come to grips with your feelings about how the move was presented to you. Part of what I heard you say you were feeling was resentment due to what you see as the arbitrariness of the whole thing, is that right?

Don: Yes. I know they think they know what's best for me, but I don't need their paternalism. I want to decide what's best for myself.

Judd: Sure you do. But don't let the way the thing was presented to you—or simply the fact that you were offered it—overwhelm you one way or another when you make your decision. Decide on the basis of whether or not the job and the move are what you want for you and your family.

Don: All right. I'll calm down and try to get a better perspective before I make a decision.

Judd: Do you have some time before you need to tell your boss your decision?

Don: He wants to know as soon as possible, of course. But he'll give me as much time as I need.

Judd: Do this, then. With your wife, weigh the advantages and disadvantages of accepting the move and then of not accepting the move.

Write them down. Then, see what you can do to compensate for any of the disadvantages you list in connection with either going or staying. After you've done that, "make a decision for a day." Think what things would be like if you followed through in the situation in the way you decided. Project yourself into that situation, for some things will be different now, regardless of whether you decide to go or to stay.

Don: That makes a lot of sense to me. And you're right; things will be different, either way.

Judd: One other thing. The apprehension, the anxiety, the butterflies in your stomach aren't likely to go away even after you've decided what to do. They'll probably stay with you for a while. Most big decisions have left me limp, tired, still a little worried even though I feel I've done the right thing and made the best choice for me. You may have the same experience. I think important decisions, once made, don't leave us exhilarated.

Don: You're right.

Judd: I'll be interested to know how you finally come out. I've had to make the same decision a few times myself.

Don: I know. Thanks for listening. I think I can approach the situation better now. I may want to talk to you again once I've talked things over with my wife.

Judd: Good. I respect and value our friendship and am always available to talk.

Don: Thanks. Thanks a lot.

The personal and emotional costs of relocating are increasingly being documented. Diane Margolis has written an important book on this topic entitled *The Managers: Corporate Life in America.*[3] The book is somewhat mistitled since it primarily discusses the feelings and perceptions of eighty-one wives of corporate managers who participated in detailed interviews conducted by Margolis. The theme of this book is the benign tyranny of the organization that employs their husbands. A tyranny that is manifest primarily in the requirement that employees move house and household upon demand.

Those who run corporations maintain that there are good reasons for periodically relocating employees: to avoid parochialism in decentralized locations, to provide visibility to those who are on their way to the top, and to encourage the dissemination of ideas and techniques. Yet, whether or not the problems caused by such frequent moves offset the benefits obtained is often an unasked question. It is a question that those who are faced with relocation, however, ask themselves. It is an important personal question that should be both asked and answered.

In this situation, Don confides in a personal friend in order to sort out his own feelings about relocating again. He is angry and resentful about even being asked to move. He feels betrayed; in a no-win situation. He believes that he must sacrifice either his career aspirations with the corporation or his family's well-being.

Judd's basic approach is to calm Don down so that they can look at the dilemma in a more rational way. Instead of paraphrasing and active listening, which would likely only cement Don's resentment, Judd provides humor. By doing this, the situation begins to look less bleak to Don. Once Don has expressed his feelings and been listened to by a friend, he has experienced the emotional equivalent of grieving. He is ready now to accept the situation as given and realistically evaluate his options.

Judd's approach emphasizes helping Don make a good decision about the choice that confronts him. Instead of focusing on problem definition, through his questions and counsel, Judd prompts Don to assess the options he has. An important bit of information that Judd provides is for Don to consider how he might compensate for the disadvantages that would be part of either moving or staying. In decision making, it is important to move beyond *identifying* limitations inherent in a particular course of action and to plan ways to *compensate* for them. This removes some of the awesomeness from big decisions. Making a decision for a day and imagining the likely consequences—positive and negative—also minimize some of the finality of decision making. Judd's approach helped Don to identify options and limitations and decide in a more rational way—by counting the varied costs of both relocating and remaining where he was.

Conclusion

Correcting, coaching, and consulting objectives and methods have been described in this chapter. These three terms have been used to describe different counseling orientations when working with people on improvement of their competence and dealing with typical problems they face. We all encounter day-to-day problems and appreciate those who are willing to listen, able to understand, and capable of helping us with them. Counseling is a cathartic function—we feel better when we've experienced it. When talking about our problems out loud, we understand them better ourselves. But counseling also has a remedial and a developmental function: we can change and improve through counseling. We can appreciate the importance of work rules, learn to do our jobs better, and get more satisfaction from our jobs through the counseling process. It is well worth the time for managers to become skilled in counseling.

References

1. Herzberg, Frederick: *Work and the Nature of Man* (New York: World, 1966).
2. Jourard, Sidney: *The Transparent Self* (New York: Van Nostrand, 1971).
3. Margolis, Diane Rothbard: *The Managers: Corporate Life in America* (New York: Morrow, 1979).

Chapter 6

Career Assessment and Development

It completely refused to run (a) when the waves were high, (b) when the wind blew, (c) at night, early morning, and evening, (d) in rain, dew, or fog, (e) when the distance to be covered was more than 200 yards. But on warm, sunny days when the weather was calm and the white beach close by—in a word, on days when it would have been a pleasure to row—the (outboard motor) started at a touch and would not stop.

—John Steinbeck
The Log from the Sea of Cortez

Steinbeck's description of an outboard motor provides an apt prelude to a discussion of career counseling in organizations. When a person has considerable potential for higher-level positions, when promotions and salary increases are available, when manager and subordinate have an open relationship—in short, whenever it is a pleasure to do so—career counseling occurs naturally and frequently. Most of the time, however, and especially when it is most needed, career counseling processes refuse to "run" properly.

Survey data confirm the need for more and better career counseling. In unpublished data that I have helped collect during the past several years from over 5000 managers in a cross section of organizations, inadequate career counseling was consistently cited as a major source of dissatisfaction. Furthermore, attitude surveys conducted in a major oil company since 1976 consistently show lack of career counseling as the predominant concern of employees at all levels of the organization despite concerted efforts by corporate managers and management development personnel to improve how and how often career counseling is done.

"The trouble with today's employees, especially our younger managers and professionals," one experienced corporate executive confided, "is that everyone is ambitious, but no one knows what they want." Typically, career counseling is regarded as appropriately informing individuals of their potential and then advising them of the best means of achieving it. Although assisting a person in deciding upon career aspirations and then providing direction in achieving those goals certainly constitute one aspect of career counseling, it is by no means all-inclusive. In fact, too often in career counseling we may misconstrue employees' concerns and believe that they simply want help in deciding "what am I going to be when I grow up?" (expressed as "What is my next job going to be and how soon can I expect it?). Understandably, managers who are placed in the position of responding to such queries feel uncomfortable and unprepared to deal with them. Representative of some of their concerns are:

> How can I tell a young, hard-charging professional supervisor what his or her next job will be? There are so many jobs that may be good for such a person, and even I don't have control over the exact next assignment. So I talk in generalities that I know aren't very satisfying to either one of us. But what else can I do?
>
> > —Functional controller,
> > major division
> > of a large corporation

> I want to encourage my "stars," but I have a lot of good people who may not "ring the bell" or "call the shots" but are vital to a productive group. I know they could go elsewhere if they wanted to scout out the market. But I don't want to lose them. How can I encourage them?
>
> > —Regional marketing manager,
> > consumer products firm

> Probably about 30 percent of the planned job changes we devised at the beginning of the year that affect any of the top 500 actually occur as planned. We spend a lot of time planning management development moves, and yet our batting average is no higher than that. How can you do career counseling in such an unpredictable environment?
>
> > —Vice president and corporate secretary
> > major multinational corporation

Each of these concerns highlights some of the more common concerns voiced by managers about why they don't do career counseling: they can't predict a next move, they lack information on available options, they don't want to fuel expectations, they don't want to discourage capable people who are not on the fast track by realistically communicating their potential. In an era when employees want more information and expect more openness concerning their careers, managers may be hard-pressed to give specific counsel and direction even when they are inclined to do so. "There are too many changeable variables," an explanation which their subordinates may interpret as evasiveness.

What's to be done?

Career Counseling—A Perspective

The term "career" suffers from too many meanings. Too often career development is regarded as the process of getting promoted, and so career counseling is viewed as ways to tell someone how to advance. Career development and counseling, however, deserve to be considered in a much broader context. In fact, the processes and activities of career counseling can be understood better if their focus is more clearly defined. Practicing managers are too often at a loss to do career counseling because they conceptualize it as informing a person of future job opportunities and optimal advancement strategies. Rather than emphasizing what people may want to *be*, such efforts should be directed at what they wish to *do* during their work life with the organization. Such a perspective suggests an entirely different framework for career counseling that is sometimes referenced in popular "career survival handbooks." This focus changes career counseling from crystal ball gazing, as it is too often regarded, to self-assessment, reality testing, and problem solving.

As noted earlier, career counseling probably occurs naturally and frequently when a manager and subordinate have an open working relationship. There are a number of recent books and articles which describe various life and career stages and how a person passes from one stage to the next.[1] But how does a person deal with the pressures and tensions in a career? When a person is frustrated by an authoritarian boss, disappointed at being "passed over" for a promotional opportunity, undecided about accepting a promotion that would require a geographical relocation, confused about career goals, or concerned about balancing personal lifestyle and professional demands, what can anyone else say or do that can help such a person better assess and come to terms with such situations?

There is a human tendency to be overwhelmed by tension and stress and to resist dealing with them. Thus, we tend to make what one observer calls "terrible simplifications."[2] When confused, disappointed, or upset, we tend to reduce decisions to "either-or" propositions. That is, we view career dilemmas as exclusive and final. With no margin for error, the pressure to make the "right" decision increases. Thus, in one case, a manager may view a promotional opportunity that requires a relocation which he knows his spouse will not welcome as choosing between "pleasing my wife or satisfying myself." Similarly, a woman in a staff meeting who perceives a remark by one of her colleagues as sexist may see the situation as requiring that she "stand up for what's right" or "ignore it since its trivial." Tension increases with the possibility of making a wrong choice. Such tension and these dilemmas are, however, unnecessary most of the time.

Difficult choices which determine how and where a person will perform at work form the substance of career counseling. The more difficult the choice, the greater the need. Like Steinbeck's outboard motor, however, things are less likely to "run" correctly when conditions are least favorable.

During the last several years I have interviewed a number of managers in a variety of organizations to better understand how effective counseling at the workplace can occur when employees are faced with difficult choices in their careers. All together, interviews have been conducted with two presidents of international banks, two state university chancellors, two presidents of major retail sales organizations, three major manufacturing company presidents, and more then fifty-five middle managers in diverse occupations about their concerns, ideas, and successes in career counseling. This group has emphasized that the problems they encounter most often that they are the least prepared to deal with involve subordinates who are confused about career goals and personal priorities, frustrated by obstacles they see in their path of career progression or self-fulfillment, or anxious about their ability to satisfy the variety of demands placed upon them. Their examples and suggestions illustrate how these concerns typically arise and how through counseling they can better be resolved.

Seeing More Clearly: How to Sort through Confused Goals and Aspirations

In an interview, one mid-level manager articulately voiced concern about the contradictions between his actions, values, and aspirations that was shared by many others talked to. "I'm 47 years old, fairly happily married for 23 years, with two children, a dog, and a large house in a good neighborhood. While waiting in the airport recently a young college kid started to talk to me and after a few minutes remarked, 'You've really got it made.' But I don't feel that way. I take home a full briefcase every night and work more weekends that I take off. Obviously, I like it, but I'm haunted by my concern that I might not be made a vice president when by boss retires. I'd think that none of my accomplishments would have been worth the daily sacrifices if I didn't get that job. I'd like to be more involved with my family, the community, even politics. But where's the time? I guess my personal aspirations are really contradictory at times."

Sorting Out Confusion

It is often assumed that people know what they want and that problems are the result of an inability to obtain desired outcomes. More often than not, however, people are confused about what they really want—especially from their work—or they want many different and conflicting things. Simply exhorting them to decide what is important to them, in such cases, is less than helpful. It is negatively self-reinforcing. People are not, as some psychologists have suggested, composed of a simple hierarchy of stable and orderly needs. They are instead, a polyglot of many things. Human needs can more appropriately be thought of as similar to the contents of a grocery bag—strewn, with no particular order. It is natural, then, to expect people to be unclear about what their real needs and wants are and how they can best be met.

It is not unusual for some employees to have a vague dissatisfaction with the organization that employs them. Ambitious employees, who want to excel and achieve, are often characterized by ill-defined goals, except for their most grandiose ones. The essence of ambition is simply a dissatisfaction with the way things are. Personal confusion, moreover, can also be the result of deliberately ambiguous lines of authority or organizational policies. In fact, organizational uncertainties seem so widespread that coping with ambiguity may be the most basic task required of us by organizations.

Confusion, moreover, can be its own reward. One can avoid taking responsibility for anything simply by resorting to this panacea. Responsibility for career planning can be placed on the organization; responsibility for ethical decisions can be passed up the pyramid; responsibility for the development of others can be neglected or seen as resting completely with the individual; all this and more can be done simply by being innocent and avoiding data gathering and decisions that would dissipate confusion. Saying "I'm not sure what I want," or "I didn't know I was supposed to do anything about it," or "I figured other people higher up in the organization had better information, so I didn't question the decision" can be wonderfully self-satisfying, to say the least.

Confusion can have many different sources, but ultimately it stems from indecision. Making decisions and choices about what is important and worth doing can dissipate the confusion that characterizes many lives. Moreover, recognizing that most decisions can be changed and modified can ease the burden of making choices. An important function of counseling is to help someone else see that nearly all decisions can be reversed, altered, or modified. Many times people are unwilling to make decisions because of their fear of being wrong. They lock themselves into their choices, hide behind them, or fail to make them. But few decisions, in fact, are irreversible or unalterable. Decisions can be remade, or situations can be altered. Moreover, making choices clarifies a position because it allows us to test our thinking and, only thereby, determine if the choice was good. Knowing that a decision was good is usually an afterthought.

Developing a work or personal values inventory can be very useful in sorting out not only what one wants to *be*, but more importantly what one wants to *do*. Too often, in looking at issues in career development or personal values, counselors have sought to help a person answer the age-old question "What do you want to be when you grow up?" This is the wrong question and approach. Attempts to answer it will likely only promote more confusion or frustration. Why? Several reasons. First of all, such a question views people as static entities, which we are not. The implicit message in the question is "You are inadequate. You don't even know what you want to be." Second, attempts to answer such a question can create expectations that are unrealistic or unattainable. But most important of all, the question tends to shift a person's attention away from examining what he or she *likes to do* and instead focuses attention on his or her *outcomes* and the *rewards*. This focus on the destination instead of the journey is the cause of much confusion and frustration.

And what if the destination is reached? In his autobiographical writing, John Stuart Mill described the nature of a particular personal depression. He was reflecting on his life and ambitions and asked himself this question: "Suppose that all your objects in life were realized; that all the changes in institutions and opinions which you were looking forward to could be completely effected at this instant: would this be a great joy and happiness to you?"[3] His answer was negative. Attaining goals brings less satisfaction than working toward them and enjoying the process.

A useful approach in sorting out personal confusion or internal conflicts is to focus on what the person *enjoys doing*. In this way, internal outcomes and personal satisfaction can be highlighted as the reward structure. In working through confusion, this counseling approach suggests that aid should be given to those seeking answers to such questions as:

- What kind of person am I?
- How do I react in pressure situations?
- What are the pluses that I have going for me?
- What can I learn about myself from noting how I relate to strangers, casual acquaintances, and friends?
- What recent experiences have I had that gave me a great deal of personal satisfaction?

It may also be useful to encourage a person in such a situation simply to make a decision, then by responding to such self-assessment questions as the following, imagine what life would be like:

- What would things be like?
- How would I feel?
- How would others view me?
- What can I do to increase the likelihood of being treated the way I think I should be?
- What can I do to continue to believe in myself?

Such self-analysis and mental rehearsal are widely used by people who have effectively integrated a wide variety of different facts of their lives. A forthcoming research report will document 15 years of interviews with about 1200 top performers in business, sports, education, medicine, and the arts which suggest that mental rehearsal is a key factor in productive functioning. This method is best employed by consciously imagining what a future situation may be like and then mentally preparing to deal with it. Some of the questions cited earlier set this process in motion to sort through contradictory career goals and assist in evaluating their likely outcomes.

Organizational life and processes are becoming increasingly more complicated. Managers and their families are redefining aspirations and goals and seeking to create a personal world that is more satisfying. Success in achieving such objectives depends on creating a personal philosophy that touches on the depth and breadth of their lives.

Frustration: Where It Begins, How to End It

"I had four major promotions in four years several years ago when I was in my thirties. I was in the highly sought after position of corporate strategic planner. I had the title and responsibilities I wanted and felt that I was sitting on top of the world. Then, the bubble burst, although the suddenness was simply my realization of what had happened. No one took my ideas seriously. I was totally frustrated. I didn't have the depth of experience in some of my earlier jobs to really talk about the subtleties of some of the things I was expected to evaluate. Regardless of how bright you are, some things only come through experience."

No one keeps statistics on managers who climb too far too fast, but the personal and organizational costs of rapid promotions can be significant. Organizations sometimes have difficulty in delicately maintaining a balance between promoting talented people quickly enough to keep them satisfied and keeping them from advancing so fast that they founder under the responsibilities of a job for which they are unprepared. Consider one case of an up-and-coming manager who was asked to salvage a floundering division. He turned things around but so alienated some of the division's best people that they either left or held back on their best ideas for fear of ridicule. He hired several consultants who rearranged reporting and budgetary relationships, but he continued to be frustrated by the untimeliness of clear operating data.

Frustration may seem to be the result of a variety of different situations: subordinates who perform incomplete analysis, colleagues who do not share data, superiors who have unreasonable or ambiguous job expectations. In recent years, a number of books, articles, and reports have appeared that describe frustrating situations on and off the job and suggest that the most effective means for dealing with people who frustrate you is to confront them openly and directly, discuss their behavior that produces a problem, and describe how you would like things to be different in order to improve things. The emphasis on openness is often compared to a relief valve on a piece of machinery: such openness gives people a chance to "blow off steam." Although such openness, expression of pent-up emotions, and confrontation may often have a cathartic effect, it can also have negative results.

My own experience in counseling dozens of parents who have physically or mentally handicapped children has given me another perspective in counseling managers who are frustrated with some aspect of their work experience. Such parents have experienced the sorrow that accompanies the loss of dreams and the realization that they may improve their situation through their efforts, but probably never substantially change it. An executive who had lived a lifetime with a mentally handicapped child had this to say about how he handled his frustrations. "I love my daughter and always have. Even though she is different from others, her wants are simple, and she is easily elated with any approximation of a wish fulfilled. Nonetheless, I sometimes resent the immediacy she often demands in expecting her needs to be satisfied and the restrictions she places on my life. I have never really 'gotten over' some of these negative feelings. I have understood them for what they are—occasional frustration—without feeling guilty about them. After I give them their due for a few minutes, I am able to dismiss them."

Frustrating feelings are most effectively dealt with by *identifying* them for what they are, *giving* them *their due* at selected times and places, and *objectifying* them so they can be assessed and channeled into productive problem solving. Reflection defuses emotions like frustration and detracts from their power and influence. The very act of *deciding* brings about personal control. Unfortunately, our language and our thinking about such strong emotions as frustration are riddled with a myth of passivity. We are "plagued" by upsetting conditions, as if by flies and mosquitoes. We are "driven" by ambition, as if by a prod. We are "paralyzed" by anxiety, as if by a powerful drug. We are "smitten," "overwhelmed," "undone," and "blocked" from our best efforts because of our *belief* that powerful emotions cannot be controlled. Like all myths, this one, too, is self-serving. Myths are strong declarations of what is "known"—until they are proved inaccurate. Yet, by accepting our own situation for what it is, we can better deal with our frustrations. By recognizing and objectifying emotions when we are unable to change external events, we loosen the hold that frustrating feelings may have over us.

Research of which I have been a part has found, through interviews, a high correlation between frustrating feelings and unrealized ambitions. More often than not, those most frustrated in their careers are those who have put themselves on a strict timetable of career development and have not yet "arrived" at their desired destination. Thus, career frustrations are not tied to fuzzy career objectives or poor career planning as some would suppose, but are instead the result of *overplanning*. When our career plans are rigid and demanding, we are going to be frustrated. Consider for instance the frustration we feel when we have arrived on time for an airplane flight and the emotion that is aroused when the plane is delayed and the agent is unsure as to when it will be available to depart. We say, in essence, to ourselves "I have arranged my life to be here at such and such a time with the *expectation* that the plane would leave on time. Now, you do *not* even *know* when it will leave!"

Overplanning and scheduling in considering career possibilities or attempting to climb career ladders without establishing expertise in appropriate functional areas may lead to problems for both individuals and organizations which employ them. Recently, an aerospace firm hired three young M.B.A.s from a prestigious business school to supervise its accounting office. Unfortunately, none of them had any experience in advanced accounting methods and, of course, knew very little about the organization and the people employed by it. Consequently, they could not spot errors or teach their subordinates where to look for problems. Eventually, one quit, one was fired, and the third transferred to a lower-level job in another department where he could learn both accounting and the company. The personal and organizational costs of moving people too far too fast can be very high.

What can managers and those who counsel them about career concerns do to avoid some of these problems? Previously conducted research based on a study of 2500 engineers in 7 large organizations has shown that sucessful people move from an apprentice to technical specialist to mentor to sponsor role regardless of their technical discipline or place in the organization's hierarchy.[4] This model provides an accurate overview of productive careers and suggests that a person who attempts to skip a stage or move to a higher stage before mastering some of the technical and psychological issues in a lower stage will probably be frustrated. Recognizing and coming to terms with who we are and what we want out of our careers is a second important aspect toward reducing career frustrations. We should become aware of the ways in which we establish deadlines and schedules for career progression that may leave us frustrated when promotions do not come as quickly as we wish or that may push us into positions we are not fully ready to handle.

It is not an easy task for a person to determine when he or she is ready for a particular promotional opportunity. However a survey of managers, mentioned earlier, produced this advice:

- "It is important not to get seduced by the money in considering a promotional opportunity. A big salary increase may be very attractive, but if you can't perform or don't like the work, it isn't going to matter very much."

- "Changing jobs too fast can get you labeled as a 'water walker' which has good and bad connotations. It not only means you are traveling too fast, but also that you are not getting your feet wet."

- "If you are only spending 12 to 18 months on a job, you may be coming up with new ideas, but you're probably not learning how to implement very well. It takes 2½ or 3 years in a position to learn how to get results and implement sustained changes that are built into organizational routines."

- "I've always asked myself some penetrating questions when offered another assignment: Why have I been chosen? Have others turned it down? Is it consistent with what I like to *do?* Am I ready for a change? What will I need to learn? Is there something special that I'll bring to the party? Just asking these questions is half the solution in determining whether a job is right for me."

When frustration results from the unfulfillment of personal aspirations, other techniques may be necessary. The unrealized aspirations of many people are a function of not counting the costs and developing an appropriate plan in order to achieve the intended goal. There are exceptions, of course: people who are functionally tone deaf who want to be musicians or those who want to possess technical expertise in some discipline but lack the necessary intelligence. But more often than not we want things for which we are not prepared to sacrifice to achieve or which we do not know how to get even if we were inclined toward such sacrifice.

The lack of fit between what people like to do and want out of their jobs and actual work requirements is another cause of frustration. Personal ambitions and the promise of monetary rewards may lure some people into accepting a job or an assignment for which they are not well-suited. Ed Schein's work on career dynamics has shown that a "technically anchored" person will see the natural interpersonal process in organizational life, such as bargaining with other work units, facing departmental conflicts, and overcoming senior manager resistance to change, as "damn politics getting in the way." Yet, another person, whose career anchor is in "managerial competence," will experience these same events positively. Such a person sees opportunities and challenges instead of frustration and roadblocks.[5]

An initial step in getting a handle on unfulfilled personal aspirations is to develop a goal statement that reflects as much individual control as possible. The more a person chooses goals that other people largely control, such as a goal to become vice president of XYZ Company, the more likely that person is to be frustrated. People free themselves and avoid frustration when they explicitly select goals over which they themselves have primary control.

Another key factor in mastering disappointment is to become aware of one's own emotional reaction to unfulfilled expectations.[6] For instance, is the frustration evoked at work handled by displacing it at home with one's spouse or children? Or do things build up until a tolerance level is surpassed? Becoming aware of how one reacts to frustrations is a key to their mastery. Counseling can be especially useful in such cases by directing this personal energy into productive activities such as assessment and goal setting instead of displacement and disappointment.

Anxiety and Demands—Making a Good Match

I'm expected to perform and do well in everything I do: at the office, in the civic groups I participate in, at my church. I'm a "take charge" kind of guy, and I like the feeling of being in control and directing things. Demands motivate me; I like to think of myself as being able to keep lots of balls in the air at once. I'm a perfectionist, I'll admit it, and probably a workaholic—so what? I enjoy what I do. That is, as long as everything's going right. I really get angry, however, when someone botches a job or fails to deliver something on time. I can't seem to help myself. I yell at my wife when dinner's not ready on time or at my daughters when their grades slip. I've dressed down many a subordinate for incomplete work, too. I know this behavior alienates me from others, but I can't seem to control it. If I suppress my feelings for a week or two, I'm like a time bomb waiting to explode.

—Corporate vice president,
major manufacturing company

A major operating norm in most organizations in today's postindustrial society is the demand for perfection or, in its alternative terminology, the fear of failure. It is not understood why this motivational influence is so dominant and widespread, but it seems to be widespread in the institutions studied and among the managers interviewed. Perhaps it is a function of the Horatio Alger mythology and the merit ethic which maintains that people prosper by their own efforts and that there is an opportunity for all to advance. Perhaps the opportunity for vertical mobility has been so visible and real for white males in American society, in particular, that failure has been especially frightening since it could not be blamed on others but had to be accepted as a personal fault.

Whatever its source, fear of failure and demands for perfection are widespread in many organizations. Their significance is that they seem to alienate managers from their personal needs and wants and impel them to avoid any characteristics associated with weakness or failure. Unbending and unyielding to their own needs and the needs of others, they rob themselves and their organizations of the dynamism that produces creative effort. A person who had risen rapidly to corporate secretary in a major conglomerate described the effect of these motivational processes in these vivid terms:

There is such a high premium placed on perfection here that innovation suffers. Innovation implies trial and error, but when there is no tolerance for error, you can bet that there will be limited trying, and less imagination. If you were to compare the situation to school, you'd say that anyone who shows up gets a "B." Those who try and succeed at something get a "B +," those who fail get an "F." There's no middle ground. I'm still trying to figure out what you get an "A" for. It's definitely not effort.

We are not suggesting that the desire to do well is bad. It is not. It can be very healthy and positive for individuals, organizations, and society. However, when it becomes a demand for perfection, it invariably generates a condition that causes people to sever themselves from everything that is not as perfect. We lose a sense of ourselves and others in the process.

The consequences to an organization of having a manager who has a "high" fear of failure can be quite severe as well. Such a manager could be expected to resist concrete performance feedback, avoid taking risks or encouraging innovation, engage in safe and predictable activities, and surround himself or herself with people who will complete observable bureaucratic chaos (however mundane or inconsequential) on time. These patterns of behavior are so obviously dysfunctional for organizational effectiveness that they do not require further elaboration. Recognizing that they stem from an overemphasis on obtaining measurable organizational results and run counter to self-appraisal and reflection is necessary in identifying ways to reduce the alienation they engender.

People who resist making changes in their lives that they acknowledge would bring them more satisfaction and a greater sense of fulfillment are not simply being negative and fearful. In our self-conceptions, we have images of ourselves that protect us from unwanted feelings and events. Giving them up initially makes us feel vulnerable and insecure. We would rather have our anxieties than none at all, because they are both familiar and personal. We've grown accustomed to them.

Once managers begin to understand the effects of the demands they place on themselves and others, they are in a position to evaluate their own personal feelings, actions, and beliefs. Effective appraisal is not easy but can be intensely rewarding. When we better understand our strengths and weaknesses, we can *improve* ourselves. When we better understand our emotional makeup and organizational processes, we can *accept* ourselves. When we better understand what is important to us individually, we can *fulfill* ourselves. One way to begin self-assessment is by recalling activities or events that have been pleasant, productive, or rewarding, then, evaluating each experience to determine *why* it is so satisfying. Talking to someone about such experiences can be particularly useful for two reasons. First, talking to someone about our concerns and hopes helps us to see them more clearly. When we acknowledge problems or wishes to someone else, we also acknowledge them to ourselves. Second, talking to someone provides a check on our own self-assessment. Others can help us see the constraints and conditions we are imposing in a situation that may be unrealistic or unwarranted.

Recognizing Constraints

Our beliefs about what can be done about a particular problem are often limited by constraints that either we or the situation imposes. Recognizing constraints imposed by a situation is important. Without doing so, we might overlook aspects that dramatically affect any solutions. Time, resources, and implementation methods always constrain the effectiveness of any solution (although their influence is often overlooked). Self-imposed constraints can also significantly influence any potential solution we may devise or decide to implement. Through the counseling process, it is possible to help others see the constraints they are unnecessarily imposing on a situation and thereby help them consider a wider range of possible solutions to a particular problem.

Ernst Beier believes that a counselor can help others see the self-imposed constraints they are placing on a situation by giving what he calls an "unexpected response."[7] We saw this in Chapter 5. Beier believes that people crave certainty and will go to great lengths to make their world as predictable as possible. For instance, when men and women say to each other, "I never want to see you again," what they may really intend is for the other person to do what he or she always does when chastised. Thus, to help someone through counseling, it is necessary to look beyond the words spoken and instead decipher the response that the person is seeking to elicit in others. This is an important key to their personal objectives. Giving an unexpected response helps those being counseled consider other objectives and other solutions besides the predictable ones. An unexpected response refocuses their thinking, motivates their problem solving, and helps their problem-solving search to be both more creative and realistic.

Although the following example is not taken from a counseling situation, it illustrates the effect an unexpected response can have in reorienting someone's thinking. According to a newspaper account, a young man went into a grocery store, pulled out a gun, and demanded that the elderly woman who was minding the store hand over all the money. The woman smiled and in a kindly voice asked, "How much do you really need, son?" Lowering the gun he replied, "$5, ma'am." She opened her purse and gave him $5 from it. He promptly left.

The usual options that are considered in cases like this are either compliance or resistance. In this particular case, an unexpected response changed the eventual outcome of the situation. In counseling, giving an unexpected response can highlight the self-imposed constraints that can be dropped once we become aware of these constraints. Sometimes a verbal message is not necessary to give an unexpected response.

Advice is often ineffective in counseling simply because the advice given is an extension of a cliché or superficial response. Without personal investment by a counselor in someone else's problem, advice means nothing. What makes advice effective is when it's least expected—like the marriage counselor mentioned earlier who asks couples why they haven't already gotten a divorce. Such a counselor is effective because few couples expect such a question. The question helps them to begin to look at self-imposed constraints.

Making It Work: Counseling Aids

Counseling is problem solving with people. It is not so much a skill as it is a set of skills, being composed of such things as listening, communicating, understanding, clarifying, thinking, helping, assisting, advising, and sharing. Counseling is not a passive function. It is more than "talking things over," although it is *not* a complicated set of procedures that must be followed correctly to avoid dire consequences. Counseling is a perspective that maintains that people often think best when they can think out loud with someone else who will test their ideas and help them be rigorous in their approach. Such reality testing, it has been found empirically, does improve the quality of problem solving.

Counseling is assisting people in the process of problem solving. It includes helping people decide. It is not deciding for people, but rather aiding people in *how* they go about deciding. Rather than telling people what they should do, a counselor points out assumptions which may be questionable, constraints which may be self-imposed, problem definitions which may be restrictive, alternatives which may be incomplete, and solutions which may not fit the problem at hand. These activities, performed in a way that encourages people to generate valid conclusions, are a reflection of the skills needed to be effective in counseling.

The reluctance of many employees to put themselves "one down" relative to a counselor often prevents them from discussing difficulties they are encountering in their work life and work relationships. They fear being taken advantage of, being used, or losing face. It is especially difficult for employees who are ambitious and who are eager to demonstrate their abilities to their superiors to admit that they are experiencing difficulties. Yet, it is often these same employees who would benefit most from consulting discussions. These employees, if drawn into a consulting dialogue, may attempt to equalize the inherent imbalance by not listening, denying the counselor's assessment of a situation, or belittling the quality of the information offered or the skills of the counselor. Such reactions occur because of the embarrassment felt when a personal weakness has been exposed. Defensiveness, such as demonstrated by the following statements, may then be expressed:

- "Your idea won't work" (because of thus and so).
- "You just don't understand. You haven't been through it, and so you really can't relate."
- "I've already thought of that, and it won't work."

Such defensiveness is a natural reaction to a threat to one's security. The imbalance that is inherent in the consulting relationship makes the potential for being taken advantage of so obvious that most people will feel a desire to reduce dependency in some way. If the counselor recognizes the occurrence of such defensive reactions and is prepared to deal with them, he or she will be more likely to return the consulting dialogue to a more even keel. If the counselor attempts to counter an employee's expressed or implied defensiveness with more pressure or additional argument, the results are likely to be self-defeating. Defensiveness is best handled by allowing the other person to express fully his or her emotions without the counselor's agreeing or disagreeing.

Responding to defensive reactions with acceptance and understanding can also assist the other person in putting the discussion on a more equal basis. Discounting can also be dealt with by turning the problem back to the person and asking, "Given your concerns, what do you think would be useful?"

Another difficult aspect of the counseling relationship is the tendency to use the discussion to seek sympathy or confirmation of a preconceived course of action rather than realistically evaluating possible alternatives. Often, people conceive of problems only in terms of solutions that are familiar to them. Rather than doing problem solving by gathering and evaluating information that may be available, they simply work backward from a solution to a problem definition.

For instance, an obvious solution to overpopulation in underdeveloped countries is to widely distribute contraceptives and information on family planning. Since the solution is so apparent, overpopulation is typically conceptualized in terms of these solutions. However, a major study of the reasons for the singular failure of family planning activities over a 10-year period had some surprising developments.

A consulting team decided to assume that Indians knew how to control the size of their families since, though the families were typically very large, most couples had fewer children than they were biologically able to have. The team decided that the real problem they faced was in understanding *why* the Indians *wanted* as many children as they did. The *reason* the Indians wanted large families became apparent after some investigation. It seems that ever since India had gained independence, the government had been able to increase the expected life span of the average adult significantly. But nothing had been done to increase the employable life span. Typical adults could be expected to live years beyond the time they were able to work.

Since India had few, and very limited, old-age pension plans that were either publicly or privately supported, most couples had to rely on their children to support them in their old age. The facts are that in India the infant mortality rate is high and generally only males work; therefore, a couple needs an average of four sons to ensure they will be adequately cared for in their old age. The consultants found that most low-income families had this very characteristic. Therefore, to ask most Indians to have fewer children was to ask them to remove their source of support and security in their advanced years.[8]

As important as it is to recognize the imbalance that is inherent in the counseling relationship, it is just as important not to overreact to it. Overreacting to an employee who has a concern by being sympathetic, coddling, overly friendly, dismissive of the responsibility the person shares in the problem, and the like can be just as counterproductive as not even recognizing the inherent imbalance in the consulting relationship. When a counselor overreacts, the situation is unlikely to change. Overreaction is exemplified in the statements which follow:

- "Gee, you've really tried hard to do the right thing."
- "It's really not your fault, and the solution would work if other people would only let it work."
- "You really have been dumped on. I don't know if I could take what you have as well as you have."

Ingratiating sentiments such as these, although intended to develop a bond between the counselor and the employee, instead only tend to emphasize the distance between their worlds. A counselor must help others deal with their own worlds and will be ineffective when he or she attempts to do otherwise. We cannot make our individual worlds free from anxiety, disappointment, and frustration. We can only learn to cope with them and minimize their effects on us and others.

A manager's ability to get involved with an employee who has a concern is a necessary part of the positive work relationship. This aspect of effective counseling is not to be minimized. However, the price of personal involvement is not dependent upon being obsequious.

William Glasser indicates that the way two strangers get acquainted is similar to the process of effective consulting.[9] According to Glasser, some of the personal attributes or qualities which promote successful outcomes include the counselor's readiness and ability to be demanding, yet sensitive; to share openly his or her own struggles, disappointments, etc.; to be genuine and not maintain an aloof stance; to allow his or her own values and perspectives to be challenged by the employee; not to accept excuses for evasion of responsible action; and to demonstrate courage by confronting perceptions and biases the employee possesses.

Summary

Fritz Roethlisberger once said that the role of the behavioral sciences is to provide people with walking sticks. These walking sticks are simplified models or maps of essential life issues. By understanding the choices that are ours to make we increase our freedom and our options. By understanding the likely consequences of our choices we improve the quality of our decision making. There are many choice points in any individual career. We can go forward or backward or even move from side to side in our career, as well as in our career planning processes. Reflecting on the possibilities that we have and considering the outcomes we want can improve the quality of our lives and the effectiveness of the organizations in which we participate.

References

1. See, for example, Douglas T. Hall, *Careers in Organizations* (Santa Monica, Calif.: Goodyear, 1976); and C. Brooklyn Derr (ed.), *Work, Family, and the Career* (New York: Praeger, 1980).
2. Weick, Karl E.: "Laboratory Experiments with Organizations," in James G. March (ed.), *Handbook of Organizations* (New York: Rand McNally, 1965).
3. Mill, John Stuart: *Autobiography* (New York: The American Library of World Literature, 1964).
4. Thompson, Paul H., and Gene W. Dalton: "Are R and D Organizations Obsolete?" *Harvard Business Review* (November-December 1976).
5. Schein, Edgar H.: *Career Dynamics: Matching Individual and Organizational Needs* (Reading, Mass.: Addison-Wesley, 1978).
6. Zaleznick, Abraham: "Management of Disappointment," *Harvard Business Review* (November-December, 1976).
7. Beier, Ernst: *The Silent Language of Psychotherapy* (Chicago: Aldine, 1966).
8. Ackoff, Russell L: *The Art of Problem Solving* (New York: Wiley, 1978).
9. Glasser, William: *Reality Therapy* (New York: Harper & Row, 1965).

Chapter 7

The Uses of Recognition and Feedback

It is clear from ordinary experience as well as from applied research that the need for people to feel positive about themselves is fundamental. Research, moreover, has shown that people are motivated to work or perform a task in a fashion consistent with their own perceptions of their competency. A person who feels capable and competent in performing a task will be highly motivated to perform in a manner consistent with those feelings. Thus, if a supervisor or manager encourages feelings of competency on particular tasks, as well as general feelings of competency in subordinates, they will be motivated to perform to the best of their ability. An employee who *feels* competent is much more likely to perform competently.

This observation may sound quite simple as a description of *why* people are motivated to work. But when trying to translate it into a prescriptive approach that shows exactly *how* to motivate people, things begin to become more complex rather quickly. In attempting to develop a pragmatic approach to improving workers' performance, perhaps nothing has captured managers' fancies quite so much as the behavior modification approach. Let's review this approach as well as several applications of it in industry and in formal work groups to better understand its assets and liabilities.

Behavior Modification

Behavior modification is not new. It is sometimes equated with learning or changing behavior itself. The basic process involves systematically reinforcing positive behavior while at the same time ignoring or exercising negative reinforcement to eliminate unwanted behavior. The entire behavior modification approach concentrates on the person's overt behavior and not on the underlying causes of that behavior. Concentrating on the outward behavior encourages managers to deal with what can be seen—the directly observable—and not worry about underlying causes or tensions or pressures a person may feel.

Although behavior modification would suggest that there are both positive and negative reinforcers which a supervisor can use to modify or shape desired behavior in a subordinate, those who have developed motivational programs based on this approach say positive reinforcement works better. Negative reinforcement, it appears, can often have unintended side effects that produce frustration instead. For instance, an employee who feels blamed for poor performance when criticized may react by being apathetic or angry as a means of compensating for what is seen as a personal attack.

For instance, one manager whom I know well believes in the importance of maintaining high performance standards and of encouraging the twenty people who work for him to meet those standards. He is not a tyrant and in fact is generally thought of as a nice guy. He provides encouragement when subordinates do well but is also swift to identify mistakes when they occur, believing that such immediate feedback will be useful in helping his subordinates correct their shortcomings. Such constructive criticism on his part is always given in private and never given in a harsh voice or an unyielding tone. Yet, this same manager is seen as a very poor boss by a majority of his subordinates. They report that he is picky, a perfectionist, and never satisfied with their efforts. Why such a discrepancy? Why, indeed. This situation can be understood by recognizing that high performance standards are insufficient by themselves as a means of stimulating subordinates and stretching them to reach their potential. Immediate feedback, especially negative feedback, even when it is descriptive and does not attack a worker personally, is not enough. Subordinates are likely to complain that "You can never please the guy" when bosses utilize such a leadership style. What is missing? Not necessarily praise and encouragement, because in the situation just cited the manager did use such positive reinforcers with his subordinates. What is missing in this situation is the boss's ability to communicate to his subordinates that he believes they are basically competent; this, coupled with his lack of accessibility to most of the subordinates, leaves them with the feeling that "he only sees us when he has something to say—other than that, he doesn't seem to notice when we're around." When subordinates are cynical, it is difficult for even good intentions to get through and have their desired effect. Another unintended but still negative effect of criticism is that employees may limit the reporting of events when things do not go right because of their fear of the consequences. As in the case of the ancient Greeks, who often cut off the head of the bearer of bad news, subordinates may distort or even not report mistakes they make if they believe that they will be severely criticized for their actions. Or subordinates may take no action even when they see a situation that needs something done because trying and failing is considered worse than not trying at all. (Subordinates can always rationalize and say "It's not my job to do something about that" just as passersby who witness a crime in the making often do as they quickly hurry on to their destination.) John and Mark Arnold have documented a number of cases where subordinates in an organization knew that something was wrong, but failed to do anything about it. Two examples:

> The president of a manufacturing company ordered work to begin on a new type of photocopying machine. Although those with direct responsibility believed the machine would take two years to build, they cooperated in forecasting that it could be developed in a matter of months. Working furiously, they managed to complete a prototype to meet their deadline. The president inspected and left the test room with assurances that it was ready for production. Shortly after [the president's] leaving the lab, however, the machine burst into flames and was destroyed.
>
> In one electronics firm, shipments were being predated and papers falsified to meet sales targets. Sales representatives had accepted the targets rather than complain for fear that they would be labeled as uncommitted. It took months before upper-level managers realized what was happening.

The basic tenet of behavior modification is that directly rewarding behavior produces the best results. Praise, approval, attention, and encouragement are examples of the most widely advocated positive reinforcers that are readily available to a supervisor or manager. A positive reinforcer works best when it helps people to feel good about themselves. For example, an employee may practice good housekeeping at a workstation because a supervisor acknowledges the employee's efforts by letting him or her know that they are important and appreciated.

Using positive reinforcers means focusing on positive aspects of performance to such an extent that negative aspects of an employee's performance are extinguished—they die from malnutrition. We are not very good at doing this in our society, either emphasizing positive aspects of performance or ignoring negative aspects. This was illustrated extremely well in a conversation between Alice and the mad hatter in Lewis Carroll's *Alice in Wonderland.*

Alice: Where I come from, people study what they are *not* [emphasis added] good at in order to be able to do what they are good at.

Mad Hatter: We only go around in circles in Wonderland; but we always end up where we started. Would you mind explaining yourself?

Alice: Well, grown-ups tell us to find out what we did wrong, and never do it again.

Mad Hatter: That's odd! It seems to me that in order to find out about something you have to study it. And when you study it, you should become better at it. Why should you want to become better at something and then never do it again? But please continue.

Alice: Nobody ever tells us to study the right things we do. We're only supposed to learn from the wrong things. But we are permitted to study the right things other people do. And sometimes we're even told to copy them.

Mad Hatter: That's cheating!

Alice: You're quite right, Mr. Hatter. I do live in a topsy-turvy world. It seems like I have to do something wrong first, in order to learn from that what not to do. And then, by not doing what I'm not supposed to do, perhaps I'll be right. But I'd rather be right the first time, wouldn't you?

Application of the principle of positive reinforcement is not restricted to direct feedback a supervisor may give to an employee. An aircraft company used this principle in the final assembly hanger of a maintenance and repair operation. Whenever an aircraft was made completely operational, bells rang and work was temporarily halted until the time it had taken to complete the overhaul could be placed on a large sign visible to all. Whenever a plane was completed in a particularly fast time frame, workers would turn to one another and voice approval of their cooperative accomplishment.

The Dilemmas of Praise

Every good manager is aware of the potential beneficial effect of feedback—especially praise. People like to know that their efforts as well as their results are appreciated. Yet, the same degree of praise often affects people quite differently. For instance, a manager who praises two subordinates in the same manner may find that one of them is all smiles and feels elated while the other scowls and walks off without saying a word. Why the difference?

In everything that we do we attempt to minimize uncertainty and impose a sense of order in our world. We like to act with some feeling of confidence and assurance so that our world in predictable. Feelings of stability and confidence require a certain degree of agreement and consistency between how well we think we did on a task and what others tell us about our performance. If we think we did a good job in writing a particular report but our boss says we did a lousy job, we will be bewildered. "What does he want?" How can I ever please him?" may reflect how we react and feel. On the other hand, if a boss compliments us for something we think was poorly done, we have a tendency to discount or depreciate the remarks by telling ourselves "It wasn't that good; what is she trying to do, pump me up, overcompensate for my hastily done job? Why doesn't she just tell it like it is?"

People have a need to feel congruence. In the earlier example of the two subordinates, the feedback was found to be congruent with the first subordinate's expectations. The praise given by the boss caused elation because it was consistent with the person's own self-evaluation of how well the job had been done and because it was seen as being basically deserved. The second employee, however, had an entirely different set of expectations about performance and a different evaluation of the results of the project.

Praise which is inconsistent with expectations sets up a situation where people are forced either to modify their own evaluation of their work or to distort, deny, or reject altogether the evaluation of someone else. Whether or not we reject our own prior experience and evaluation or that of someone else depends on two primary factors: the esteem we hold for that person and the incremental difference between the person's evaluation and our evaluation of our work.

How a person decides what to do with praise is well-illustrated in Elliot Aronson's book, *The Social Animal*.[2] Aronson found in repeated experiments that when a person giving praise was a credible source, people accepted or rejected the praise given to them only if it was comparatively close to their own view of their efforts. Aronson found, however, that if he could get people to evaluate their own performance first and then get a credible source, someone in an authority position, to evaluate it a little bit better, then the people would change their own evaluation, accept the higher evaluation, and be motivated to perform at that higher level. It was clear after repeated experiments that people consistently increased both their personal standards and their desire to perform at higher levels following this pattern of praising. Aronson calls this the "gain effect."

Steadily increasing praise is more appealing than bestowing lavish praise or attempting to "hype" someone up, because it continually presents a message that causes people to modify only slightly their own expectations and views regarding their performance. As long as positive feedback increases in moderate increments, the receiver will probably not view it as seriously incongruent with personal beliefs. Thus, it is credible. However, this view also suggests that praise that is nothing more or less than what a person expected will fall flat. It will neither motivate nor be depreciated. A supervisor who gives only what a subordinate expects will be greeted with nonchalance. Such positive feedback will have no effect. Thus, to summarize the gain effect, four interrelated concepts about praise need to be remembered and applied by managers in order to get a good rate of return on praise invested:

1. People tend to view feedback in light of their expectations.
2. Praise tends to go flat once a person comes to expect it.
3. Too much or too little positive feedback will have no effect. It is necessary to determine an employee's evaluation of a task first in order to eventually get the beneficial results of praise.
4. Noticing and praising small acts by employees slightly in excess of what an employee expects raises an employee's anticipation level above what the employee thinks possible. Thus, a small gain over what a person believes is due makes praising effective.

How to Give Feedback

It is difficult as a manager to play the dual role of coach and judge which is generally required in most organizations. Typically, a manager evaluates performance in order to determine salary increases or determine who will get the next promotion. Such evaluations, unfortunately, may carry over into day-to-day work relations where a manager consistently plays the role of judge and limits interactions with subordinates to critiques of their work. It is unfortunate because people at work need direction and camaraderie as well as an understanding of what the boss wants. Many bosses provide none of these, while effective managers respond to each of these needs.

Barrier: Evaluative Feedback

Only the best managers can handle the difficult human situations that call for understanding and negotiation. Others shy away from confronting the performance problems of their employees; in some offices, conspiracies can even develop to delicately avoid "people problems." These managers may have genuinely tried to talk with problem employees about their deficiencies, only to have been rebuffed. This hypothetical vignette describes an all too frequent attempt by managers to give employees performance feedback.

Manager: Look, Walt, how many times do I have to tell you not to send in a report that's incomplete. Now take it back and rework it until you've finished.

Employee: Wait a minute, Carol, I've got a million things to do around here. I can't read your mind. How do I know what you want?

The manager may walk away from this situation thinking "Walt can't take suggestions without getting mad," while the employee may walk away muttering "Carol never explains what she wants and then criticizes when things aren't done the 'right' way." Perhaps both are right. Even though the manager may have had good intentions, the results she wanted to achieve may never have materialized because of her methods, and her "suggestions" may have seemed to Walt to be arbitrary instead of helpful.

Many times, essentially positive intentions of being helpful and constructive fail to be accurately translated into actions because of a lack of interpersonal skills. As a result, instead of yielding more productive and satisfied employees, managers' efforts to improve things produce only discontent and dissatisfaction. Why? Because they use evaluative feedback methods. Such methods, the "if you know what's good for you" kind, are bound to produce resentment rather than commitment, regardless of a manager's intentions. What a manager actually says or intends is less important in interpersonal matters than what an employee hears. What can managers do, then, to communicate their intentions more completely, especially in situations where they are trying to correct a performance problem? Plenty.

Gateway: Descriptive Feedback

People need to know what is expected of them if they are to perform adequately. They also want to know when they are not performing properly, but they want to know in a way that does not force them to swallow their pride or lose their self-respect. Employees need to be told in an acceptable manner if they are not performing well. Otherwise, they will be resentful of any feedback a manager may give regarding their job performance.

One manner for giving feedback to employees that is generally acceptable to people is known as an "I message." I messages are an effective communication tool because they simply inform employees of the consequences of their actions rather than judge the actions or motives. There is even a formula for sending an I message:

I _____ (feeling) when you _____ (behavior) because it _____ (impact).

To deal with unproductive behavior, all a manager needs to do is fill in the blanks. For instance, in dealing with an employee who has had a series of absences due to personal emergencies in recent months, the manager could send the following I message:

I am troubled (feeling) by the seven absences you have had in the last 6 months (behavior) because it has created a burden on others who have had to do your work as well as their own (consequences). I want you to know that when you miss work, it affects all of us.

This formula can be used as a guide for confronting unacceptable behavior in a variety of situations. This is particularly true if the manager focuses on understanding the behavior of the employee and on sharing information instead of on attempting to judge personality traits or give advice.

On the other hand, managers may desire feedback on how their employees view them. Such sensitive information is not easily offered but can be extremely valuable. A manager can do five things to encourage feedback:

1. Affirm that it is wanted
2. Identify specific areas in which feedback is needed
3. Set aside time for planned feedback sessions
4. Use silence to encourage the flow of information at feedback sessions
5. Reward people for good information, even if it is unpleasant

Getting and giving feedback are valuable skills that every effective manager practices. Several methods are appropriate for stimulating such feedback, including one-to-one discussions, group meetings, and casual conversations. Feedback is such an integral part of the management process that every manager should develop methods for getting and giving useful feedback.

Ways to Recognize Others

Recognition is more than giving someone a pat on the back—as important as that is. It is a means of providing what one management consultant describes as "vertical job loading,"[3] that is, allowing a person to assume increasingly more challenging tasks and to obtain the inherent benefits which accrue from achievement and responsibility.

Recognition is a natural by-product of the following kinds of things which a supervisor might do which tend to elicit the response indicated from subordinates:

PRINCIPLE 1: Removing some controls while retaining accountability.

RECOGNITION: ("Hey, my supervisor must think I'm doing okay if I'm being given more job freedom.")

PRINCIPLE 2: Increasing the accountability of people for their work.

RECOGNITION: ("Finally, my supervisor will be able to see what kind of a job I've been doing all along.")

PRINCIPLE 3: Giving a person a complete natural unit of work; i.e., module, division, area, etc.

RECOGNITION: ("That's right, I work in section 4B and proud of it." "Now when I go home at night I will know just what I've accomplished today.")

PRINCIPLE 4: Making periodic reports directly available to the workers rather than just to the supervisor.

RECOGNITION: ("Gee, look how well we did last month." "Hey, they know that I did that!")

PRINCIPLE 5: Introducing new and more efficient tasks not previously handled.

RECOGNITION: ("My boss must really trust me.")

As these examples show, recognition is often communicated most when nothing is said. However, verbal praise, sincere and appropriate, is certainly a part of giving recognition. It is an activity that costs practically nothing, but often yields high rates of return.

People at work want opportunities for purposeful action and self-advancement. Jobs are important not only in and of themselves but also in terms of the status and recognition they provide. One of the first questions someone typically asks of a stranger is "What do you do?" Since the kind of job a person has is the major means of maintaining self-esteem, it is also the major means by which motivation can be enhanced.

The amount of opportunity people see in their jobs has a direct relationship to their job performance, according to Rosabeth Kanter, a Yale University researcher.[4] She has found that people low in opportunity tend to lower their aspirations, become less engaged with or committed to work, and behave in ways that usually make them look to others as though they are not suitable for promotion. High opportunity has the opposite effect of encouraging people to adopt attitudes and behaviors that will further the interests of the company to which they belong.

A situation where changing the opportunities available to a group of employees increased performance took place in a large chemical company. In a research laboratory, technicians were given the responsibility for documenting research reports and for training laboratory assistants. Those who developed proficiencies in analyzing and evaluating data were assigned as apprentices to the research scientists and allowed to develop professional competencies. Those who showed an aptitude for developing other people were given increased managerial responsibilities and allowed to become supervisors. By simply removing the lid from advancement opportunities and creating dual career paths, the company changed the performance of lab technicians dramatically.

It is easy to provide recognition and opportunities to an organization's superstars. Such people tend to get the status and recognition which they deserve. Yet, the merely good performers, who are not quite as good as the best, tend to go unnoticed. What is done for them? Unfortunately, little is done for them in many companies, and so they often do less than they are capable of doing.

How to Give Feedback on Performance

The importance of on-the-job feedback is almost universally recognized. Everyone realizes that good job performance must be noticed if it is to continue, and poor job performance must be corrected if it is to change. However, the application of this idea in most organizations works against sustaining the motivation of employees. Typically, feedback is given in such a way that the personal satisfaction or dissatisfaction to be derived from work behavior is denied the employee.

As a specific example of feedback that does not enhance motivation and feedback that does enhance it, consider a worker who successfully completes a complicated task in an efficient manner. What does the boss do? If he or she says, "I'm pleased that you did such a good job; keep it up, that's the kind of work that I like to see done," who is being rewarded? Not the worker, but the boss. The boss is the one who is happy, and who has, in essence, been complimented. If, on the other hand, the boss notices a job well-done and says, "My, that's fine work—you must feel a real sense of accomplishment," it is the employee, not the boss, who is reinforced. By recognizing performance in this way, the boss reinforces the employee's own feelings of satisfaction and lubricates the person's internal generator.

Most managers are aware of the potential for positive impact when they give feedback to employees. They know that any message affecting people's feelings about themselves—verbal or nonverbal, formal or informal—is going to have consequences for future interpersonal relations and performance. The best impact, moreover, will be achieved when good performance is noticed by reinforcing the employee's own feelings of satisfaction and accomplishment. Poor performance can be corrected in the same way—by noticing it and simply acknowledging that the employee undoubtedly finds it unsatisfactory as well.

Sometimes, however, that is the only feedback that some employees get. If so, they may realize that they are not doing a good job, but may not know how to improve. If this is the case, training is necessary. And the best way that people learn is by getting some of the positive feedback described previously.

Managers will notice increases in motivation and performance when they reinforce people's innate satisfaction from a job well-done. Mistakes are less likely when such feedback is consistently given because people naturally want to succeed and do well; mistakes also decrease when people are reinforced for doing well. Those mistakes which do occur are more likely to be remembered and not repeated in the future. It is the nearest thing to a performance insurance policy that is available.

References

1. *Wall Street Journal*, June 5, 1978, p. 9.
2. Aronson, Elliot: *The Social Animal* (New York: Viking, 1972).
3. Hackman, J. Richard, and Greg R. Oldham: *Work Redesign* (Reading, Mass.: Addison-Wesley, 1980).
4. Kanter, Rosabeth M.: *Men and Women of the Corporation* (New York: Basic Books, 1979).

Part III

Organizational Processes

Chapter 8

Team Building: Potential, Pitfalls, and Prospects

"Nothing fails like success" was the central conclusion reached by Dean Inge from his reflection on the record of civilization's history. More than just a clever paradox, this insight finds only too vivid confirmation in contemporary society. Nearly every ideal that liberal reformers battled for at the turn of the century has been achieved: universal suffrage, compulsory education, workers' protection, social insurance, increased incomes, and cheap transportation. Yet in spite of this success, almost every institution in society is "in trouble." In fact, a 1971 survey of college students revealed that almost 62 percent felt that American society is "sick." Most surveys don't indicate things have improved in the last 10 years, either.

Numerous books, articles, and broadcasts entreat those in charge to change their ways, but they fail either to operationally define the problems or to offer concrete suggestions for improvement. Leaders and managers, however, are judged on performance—not promises. As managers face the clash of new values on their current perceptions, they often find that accustomed behavior is inadequate. Bottom-line measures and T account balances are incomplete means to accommodate the uncertainty they face. Increasingly, the manager who can motivate others to achieve performance goals as well as to strive for them is the manager who is effective.

It is not enough for managers to be able to write reports and balance the books and make sales projections. They must know something about the delicate harmony that people who work together inevitably achieve and how not to disrupt the balance by applying formulated human relations techniques that are irrelevant to the situation. Prescriptions need to be saved for the pharmacy and not applied at the factory. Today's managers need to know and differentiate between employees.

Take for instance the work of a paper plant in Michigan that I recently investigated. Of 163 active employees, 53 were *over* 60 years of age, while 48 were *under* 30. Notice the diversity that typifies the comments of several young workers whom I questioned.

> "A lot of us young guys work in converting where you can only count on working 5 days a week. That makes it rough to earn enough to meet payments." —A 29-year-old employee

> "Whether the company wants me to have a day off or not, I'll have a day off." —A 30-year-old employee

> "The old guys care about their pensions. I care about what's in my pocket." —A 26-year-old employee

> "I do this job so that I can make enough money to do what I want." —A 28-year-old employee

The antagonism in the plant between young and old workers and the different rewards sought individually and collectively make the prospect of employee satisfaction difficult. Senior workers in the plant expressed some hostility about their junior counterparts who were more assertive than they thought necessary. Said one longtime employee:

> "Young guys don't know what it is to work. I worked 12 years before I could even afford a cheap car. Nowadays, these young fellows want both time and money. The young men really scare me." —A 55-year-old employee

Another older employee corroborated this perception of his younger peers.

> "The younger guys have a 'what the hell' attitude. The only thing that interests them is money and vacations." —A 58-year-old employee

Such diverse conditions and diversified characteristics are more common than unusual in today's commercial landscape. The geography of most factories is less homogeneous than every before, and potential conflicts are fueled by individual workers' expectations about what they want and what they think they should get from a job. While some employees of this paper plant admitted that they slowed down on the job just so that they could get overtime, others complained that they were required to work overtime too often. Any manager who responds to such a situation by throwing up his or her hands and saying, "You just can't please them, no matter how hard you try!" is giving a grossly inadequate response. Can anything else be expected from a trained and educated work force besides diversity?

Today's work force has expectations that have increased geometrically during the past few years. This rise of expectations as well as subsequent civil rights legislation has meant more opportunity for groups such as blacks and women. Racial and sexual integration has confronted contemporary managers with problems undreamed of two decades ago.

Racial tension in a finishing plant which I recently visited in Atlanta, although described as "amazingly cool" by the plant manager, was, nonetheless, a concern to many. Recently, a black worker on the third shift shot and permanently paralyzed a white supervisor in an incident termed by onlookers as "nonracial." A short time later, a black man with a knife threatened harm to a white man "if he didn't speak to me like he was talking to a man." Since then, says the industrial relations manager, "It is known that many employees carry guns or knives."

The implications for employee morals in such a situation are fairly clear. The mutual respect and trust necessary for an operation's effectiveness are almost nonexistent. This is affirmed by the industrial relations manager who noted that a "foreman out there at night is really alone. If a white had to discipline a black, or a black reprimand a white, and tempers flared, you never know what the hell might happen."

The problems of the Atlanta finishing plant are not even confined to the black-white issue. The increasing number of female employees has produced, according to at least one supervisor, a startlingly higher rate of absenteeism. A young member of management also commented on the attitude of female employees to the lower wages generally received by women. "They're not militant feminists, but they do notice." The operations manager further mused that "The females will probably demand more attention and will put on more pressure than the blacks. We've already had women file sex discrimination grievances."

To be effective the person in a contemporary supervisory role must be as cognizant of these industrial trends as of the fluctuations of the national economy. Technology may have made some tasks easier, but it is outside the realm of others. No computer program has yet been devised that gives reasonable answers to such issues between people on the job as have been described.

People are simply less willing to receive directives from superiors or obey what appear to them to be arbitrary rules. There seems to be what some have called an "obsolescence of authority." "A hurricane is blowing," writes organizational theorist Eli Ginzberg, and the eye of the hurricane is the "unwillingness of many individuals to accept the authority of established institutions to prescribe their goals and behavior."

The indispensable ingredient which today appears most needed is the ability of individual managers to perceive the aspirations of others, discern the realistic limits of possibilities, and select the line of advance that holds the greatest promise of success. Gandhi's classic bus example, that a leader is like a bus driver who can take diversionary routes but may stay pointed in the right direction, is still relevant. Any leader or manager must retain the consent of subordinates in order to perform necessary tasks successfully. Any time followers refuse to acknowledge a leader's power, that person cannot perform optimally. In industry, if consent is exacted instead of developed, workers will retaliate with rate restriction or sabotage.

Enter Team Building

It is precisely this issue of power and its proper exercise that has provided a basic need for activities like team building and affiliated offshoots like "quality circles," "self-managed work teams," and other methods and techniques of participative management. Team building emerged as a popular tool for workplace management in the mid 1960s when college students were demanding more of an influence on the college campuses and moved into the world of work with similar expectations. Simultaneously—and not coincidentally—management advisers and organization development (OD) practitioners were emphasizing the practical value of group decision making. During the decade of the 1960s several new and related management axioms were formulated, tested, and developed. It seems that these ideas could be applied in almost any setting and produce desired results. These axioms maintained:

- Involvement is a precondition to commitment; people become involved through seeing their ideas become part of their work and work environment.

- Managers should act like team leaders and coaches; management is a facilitating or developing role rather than a directing role.

- Work groups have the necessary capacity to cope with their own problems provided they are aware of both of these things (capacity and problems).

- Employees are innately cooperative and self-actualizing, preferring the chance to exercise a degree of control over their world.

- Typical hierarchical organizations and their inherent trend toward more formal rules and dysfunctional bureaucratic behavior can become more effective and functional by eliminating status distinctions and emphasizing interpersonal trust and openness and self-disclosure.

Since many of these positive humanistic values have an intrinsically strong appeal and were supported by specific research studies, those who opposed their implementation were often criticized as insecure. In some organizations, they were described as "basically authoritarian" and "threatened" by such power-sharing ideas. This is not to say that team-building methods were widely used in industry or public organizations during this period. Clearly, such was not the case then, nor is it true 20 years later in the 1980s, although the application of team-building methods now is much more refined and the benefits of the approach easier to describe. Although team building as a management tool may not have been widely utilized, the *rationale* for its use nevertheless was clearly articulated and well-supported. It held the promise of providing a means of sharing power, motivating employees, improving the quality of decisions, and effectively managing the diversity increasingly characteristic of the workplace. This is not to suggest that responsible OD practitioners or forward-thinking managers see team building and related participative management techniques as a panacea to workplace ills. Clearly, such was not the case, although some "promoters," then as now, advocated such a position. However, such techniques were seen as having the *potential* for resolving a host of problems and concerns.

Trends Prompting a Reassessment

As with any model or theory, with continued use and application it becomes clearer and clearer what works, what does not, and why. Models and theories in the management arena are constrained, however, by factors and conditions unfamiliar to those in other disciplines: the subject is changing so often that it is difficult to generalize in drawing conclusions from research efforts. Employees in a small, paternalistic office machines company in the southern United States have considerably different workplace expectations and interests than those working in a unionized steel mill in the northeastern part of the country. Their histories on and off the job are different at all organization levels, and their interests, beliefs, and predispositions about their workplace roles also vary. For instance, Leonard Pearlin, a National Institute of Mental Health Fellow, recently conducted interviews with more than 2300 adults in the Chicago area regarding how they cope with pressures and strains on the job, in their marriages, with their families, and in other stressful situations. Overwhelmingly respondents said they were more likely to deal openly with family-related problems and ignore or avoid confronting work-related stresses. Would the same result be obtained in San Francisco?

This study raises the question of the practicality of openness—an important team-building valve—in modern organizations. As a principle, the importance of accurately disseminating good information–up, down, and through an organization—is unarguably important. Especially in large organizations, accurate information is often one of the scarcest of resources. But how "open" can employees reasonably be expected to be? How open should they be?

An illustration may help provide some perspective to this question. In one large organization a project manager was urged by his boss to conduct a team-building session. Although initially resistent, he finally consented. He conducted the session with the aid of an outside consultant and received some very negative feedback on his "autocratic manner" despite his brilliant insights and assistance on technical matters. The manager was devastated. Within months he had resigned from the large company and accepted employment with a consulting firm where he could do more technical work. The mid-level manager who had insisted on the program was dismayed. He felt he had lost an employee who was technically brilliant by trying to make his management style more participative. The mid-level manager was more than willing to accept the project manager's "excess" if he thought he was choosing between a desired management style and continued employment.

The openness that is advocated as a part of team building is sometimes compared to a relief valve on a piece of machinery—it provides a chance for people to "blow off steam." Thus, the metaphors we have for reducing workplace frustrations refer to "getting something off our chests," "letting it out," or "having an emotional release." They all suggest that things "build up" unless expressed and that expression alone is cathartic. Yet, if we think about it, each of us can probably recall times where the more we talked about something, the more emotional we became. We see people who gossip and spread rumors who do not seem to have strong feelings reduced or eliminated through their expression. In fact, sometimes "talking things out" bolsters our beliefs on a topic. Instead of blowing off steam, we take on more. Again, this is not to say that talking things out doesn't provide some sense of catharsis at times, but not always. There are some *conditions* that make a session designed to produce more openness effective and some which work at cross-purposes to that objective. But openness should not be an end unto itself—at least, it can produce some negative results when it is given such a place. It is not necessary that everyone like each other or the boss in order to function effectively as a work group. Cooperation and trust are more a function of *knowing* what others in a work group are like and what they *expect* in a work relationship. Trust is difficult to develop in many large organizations that rotate employees through developmental assignments in different work groups and geographical locations. This is because people don't stay in a position long enough to be well known by their working associates. The issue in such work teams is not that the boss mistrusts employees or vice versa so much as that each is unknown to the other. Expectations are unclear, and so people are continually trying to sort out relations, establish predictability, and maintain some routine. Additionally, managers at the top of such organizations view the lack of continuity in positions with some concern and so impose more external controls on those at lower levels in the organization to ensure that work is completed as desired. As one manager said to me, "It's not that I don't trust those folks, but they keep asking for guidelines and manuals. Since so many people in our organization spend less than 2 years in a job, they want something concrete when they go to a new assignment that says what to do. So, like the military, we impose more external controls."

Team Building—Redirection

With additional research and experience some important trends have emerged which allow team-building activities to be more realistically appraised. Twenty years ago, team-building approaches were not very widely used or disseminated. With their more general use and acceptance, assessment can be more forthright. At one company several years ago a catalog of team-building activities under way at twenty-six separate work locations was published describing methods, results obtained, and necessary conditions for effectiveness. Major evaluation efforts by academicians such as David Bowers, at the University of Michigan, and George Strauss, at Berkeley, have also shown that by planning and creating the right conditions, team building can produce positive and lasting change. More research is needed, of course, to continue to identify "action levers" that make team building effective, but some generalizations can be made.

Focus

In early team-building efforts, confrontation and openness were often viewed as ends unto themselves. They are only methods, however, of achieving other objectives and require appropriate training so they *can* and *will* (two separate dimensions) be used on the job. Initial confrontation leads to awareness, which must in turn lead to new skills and consideration of different ways of doing things revealed through confrontation. Team building can prove both threatening and dangerous to people who surface their own inadequacies and also to those at the receiving end of hostile emotions. The borderline between useful feedback and simply "getting back" at someone—psychologically battering them—is a fine one and deserves to be closely monitored.

The more team building focuses on *behaviors* of work group members and on organizational structure problems, the more successful such efforts will be. This *task* focus can be easier for all participants to take since it deals with observable events and avoids "amateur psychology." This may seem obvious on the surface, but in one organization that I have worked with, "process skills" were emphasized so much that no meeting could be called without someone serving as a "process consultant" and the meeting turning into an extensive team-building session following completion of the agenda. Consequently, people felt they were "continually walking on eggs" in discussing work items and overreacted to the desirable objective of reaching consensus in problem solving and decision making.

Scope

The compatibility of team-building interventions and more general organization development activities is natural. In many instances, the two go hand in hand. But not necessarily, and unfortunately, sometimes managers and those who advise them on such activities in the words of one observer, "bite off more than they can chew." Thomas Hartley, of Union Carbide, has asked, "Why, if OD and team-building efforts are so good and innovative and right, do they fail so often?" He cites concerns among the management staff and cutbacks in the professional staff who worked in this area in such companies as Boise Cascade, American Airlines, Eastern Airlines, Corning Glass, and Union Carbide in the mid 1970s as examples that something is not working as it should.

OD at a major oil company has gone through similar reassessments. At one point in the late 1960s, and early 1970s, managers didn't talk about OD. It was suspect. Widespread internal publicity had been given to a number of wide-ranging activities that promised much more than they delivered. It is very difficult to do "large-system organization change," and ambitious efforts often get waylaid for a variety of reasons. Sometimes people who want to "change" organizations don't understand the underlying technological and logistical requirements well enough to assess what is really necessary and what is not. So, when such internal change agents are fired and external consultants do not have their contracts renewed, they complain that it was because they attacked a "sacred cow" when in reality they were about to sterilize a prize bull. They just couldn't tell one from the other.

So how could OD be anathema at a company in 1972 and 5 years later a catalog of internal team-building interventions be published? Partially, the technology of a fledgling science continued to improve. Partially, "bite-sized" efforts were made instead of attempts to mass-produce organizational change and flood the landscape with it. In particular, the OD axiom of "ensure top management support" was abandoned, and emphasis was placed on working local problems at local facilities. What is needed from top management is the freedom to operate, to function in ways that fit the particular demands of a plant or district or work group. Top management wants results and in most instances is willing to tolerate a wide variety of methods—leading to that end. Obtaining top management endorsement for such efforts, moreover, may politicize them in ways that are counterproductive. Working at the middle levels in an organization is where the greatest needs exist and where managers often are most inclined and encouraged to seek innovative ways to manage their human resources.

Emphasis

One of the major indicators of the quality of employment is the extent to which people are involved with their jobs and their work. In fact, a positive relationship has been found between work involvement and such related factors as high job satisfaction and morale and positive individual work output. Unfortunately, attention has been concentrated too narrowly on "satisfaction" as the only type of attitude that should be measured and dealt with. "Work involvement" is a separate dimension from job satisfaction and is a measure of the degree to which people see their job as a central life interest or positive measure of their stature and status. It has been found that people who see work itself as an important activity are much more productive and much more likely to build positive relationships at the workplace irrespective of their job satisfaction at a given point of time. Developing high "work involvement" is related to job satisfaction, but the emphasis is very different. The first step in understanding these relationships is to stop putting the satisfaction cart before the performance horse, so to speak. It is more accurate to think of satisfaction as something that *results* from good performance. Successful people are motivated people, and a manager should strive to help people be successful by acquiring the confidence and competence to do their jobs well, which in turn leads to job satisfaction. There are many opportunities for people to get positive reinforcement from their everyday work situations. A primary management function is to identify and successfully use these opportunities and to get other members of the work group to reinforce such results through positive social support. This emphasis of looking for ways to improve work group efficiency and individual competence rather than job satisfaction per se is an important aspect of effective team building. It doesn't change the technology of team building that has been developed in the last 20 years, but it does affect the content—what is considered "grist" for the mill rather than the mill itself. Of course, the size of the grist requires adjustments in the grinder, but the process remains basically the same.

Summary

Team-building activities have been and will continue to be an important managerial tool not simply because they provide a means for employees to participate in what happens at the workplace but also because they provide a means to test agreement on work objectives, develop social support, and respond to people's desires for inclusion. Most people enjoy the interaction they have at work, and research suggests that team-type jobs are better jobs because they encourage the sharing of information. In a changing and increasingly diverse society, it is important for every organization to step back periodically to assess its mission, goals, and methods. In their most modest forms, team-building activities provide a well-defined vehicle for making such assessments. It is, after all, a process of inventory taking that deals with critical organizational dimensions that are ofttimes overlooked.

Chapter 9

Clarifying and Establishing Expectations: A Management Function

The inscription "know thyself" appears above the entrance to the ancient Temple of Apollo at Delphi. Although this admonition has been repeated often in the past twenty or so centuries, there appears to be a general resistance to this process. It can be difficult for a person to find out what really makes himself or herself tick, to realistically appraise past and present feelings, beliefs, and aspirations. However, uncovering these roots of who you are and the reasons why you define yourself as you do is crucial to your improvement. Self-awareness, self-insight, or "getting in touch with yourself" is central to almost every current theory regarding healthy personality functioning, for a lack of self-understanding leads to such undesirable results as insecurity, fear, and the atrophy of abilities, talents, and capacities.

Persons who have a restricted sense of who they are, and who have avoided insight into their personal motivations and interpersonal functionings, are likely to feel that they are victims of forces which they can neither understand nor control. They will probably find themselves doing things about which they later remark "What ever made me do that?" Have you ever remarked, after a heated exchange with another person, "I don't know what came over me. I don't know why I did that." Many are the regrets which stem from a lack of self-understanding.

Such incidents may cause people to be so apprehensive regarding the control of their emotions or actions that they avoid opportunities for growth and development. Their fears, their confusion, their apprehensions can all combine and affect self-esteem and self-confidence. We may want to change or improve so as to be more in control of our emotions and workplace lives, but do not know where to begin or what to do. Especially if we are supervisors or managers, we want to be able to influence others positively to improve and perform as capably as possible.

There is an increasingly large body of research and writing on how people change and, in particular, how organizational processes contribute to or inhibit such change. A common theme inherent in this research is that the behavior, beliefs, attitudes, and values of an individual are all firmly rooted in the groups to which he or she belongs and looks to as support structures.[1] One's aspirations, orientation, and productive or nonproductive functioning are shaped and sustained by group membership. It is apparent from this research as well that groups are not only the *target* but also the *medium* of change in either personal or organizational development.

It is also apparent from these same research sources that productive functioning hinges upon the self-evaluation or self-esteem of people individually and collectively in any enterprise. This self-esteem, contrary to a popular misconception that it is the result of a warm, supportive environment, depends instead on some important factors. Foremost are the repeated experiences of success or failure on tasks that the person sees as matters of central importance. It is apparent that we do not feel good about ourselves as a prerequisite to achievement and increased self-esteem, but rather, feeling good is the result of achievement and high self-esteem. It is important to appreciate the nature of this relationship in order to better understand how to improve ourselves and influence others.

Groups and Roles

Phillip Zimbardo, a professor at Stanford University, conducted a study that on the surface has some disturbing connotations, but upon reflection, contains some important implications for self-development and human resource management. Zimbardo conducted an experiment with a group of school children in which he asked them to play the role of mock guards and prisoners in a simulated prison setting. Although these people were chosen because they were normal on a series of psychological tests given to them, they began to act in unusual ways after just a few days in the prison simulation.

The mock guards became increasingly hostile and domineering in their treatment of the "prisoners," while the prisoners reacted to this overt display of power with signs of emotional distress, and eventually with dependency. Although the experiment was originally planned to last for 2 weeks, it was canceled after only 6 days because of the observed changes in behavior of both "guards" and "prisoners."[2]

How was it possible for these students, chosen for their parts by the flip of a coin and without training or instruction, to slip so easily into the roles they represented? They had learned from television, movies, books, and other sources what it meant to control and exercise power over the lives of others. They did not have to be told *how to act* once they understood their roles because of their perception of what their roles entailed.

The primary implication of this study is that we behave and act to a large extent in a manner consistent with what is expected of us in a group setting. We are, in large measure, what we think other people think we are. We act out roles in our jobs, in our homes, at the bowling alley, at church, and elsewhere consistent with the image we customarily maintain in such settings. It is true that we have a great deal of choice about whether or not to participate in a particular group or organization, but once we have so chosen, group norms and expectations powerfully influence our behavior.

Role Expectations—A Team Approach

Sometimes because of limited interaction patterns, or inexperience, or changing job pressures, organizations in which people work send out confusing or contradictory messages about what is expected.

A work team forms around a task that requires the cooperative efforts of more than one person; this is task interdependence. Every member of any team possesses certain skills, expertise, perceptions, and perspectives which differ from other team members. To what degree and in what manner these individual characteristics are meshed largely influence the team's effectiveness. Too little correlation and integration can result in role ambiguity or group conflict, while too much cohesion can result in "groupthink"—explicit agreement camouflaged by private, unvoiced concerns.

Task interdependence and the varied nature of individual characteristics require a basic understanding of how certain tasks will be performed by team members. A clear and agreed-upon understanding of what each member's role is requires a similar clarity and agreement of how each person should perform the various tasks incumbent in his or her position. Besides information, then, which is the issue inherent in the question of role just mentioned, everyone needs to know the required skills pursuant to task requirements and be able to identify the inherent *expectations* of upper-level managers concerning performance.

Formal written job descriptions are useful as a starting point in deciding who does what and how well but are insufficient for several reasons. First, they tend to be general in their focus, describing general duties rather than specific behaviors. Second, they do not account for the changing nature of either the positions or their occupants. Third, they do not communicate the specific expectations of immediate supervisors.

Individual team members are left on their own to find out in some way *how* they and other team members should go about on a daily, monthly, and yearly basis fulfilling their responsibilities. Sometimes team members may get conflicting messages from peers or associates concerning how they should perform their jobs. They may even get conflicting messages from their bosses who, by the areas in which they actually place their priorities, contradict their stated priorities; it seems, people often communicate most when they think they are communicating least. What supervisors actually *say* may matter less than the way in which they *behave.*

These conclusions about how a team member should operate constitute a set of role expectations. However, what individual supervisors communicate by their behavior or apparent priorities may not coincide with what they had intended to communicate either by their actions or by their conclusions. Often a team member may perceive priorities which are more partial than actual; that is, a team member, because of limited perspective or interaction, may have a fake or incomplete picture of priorities of the company. Moreover, a supervisor may not be very proficient at translating intentions into actions and so may communicate an unintended message.

The behavior of individuals while on a team is, in part, a function of their own expectations of what they think they should do. They have personal expectations of their primary task responsibilities (e.g., "I should sign all purchase requisitions") as well as expectations concerning their relationship to other members of the team (e.g., "I should not be the one to ensure that X gets X's work done"). These expectations are residual or inherent in the way the individuals define the positions which they occupy.

Personal behavior is also influenced by the expectations which others hold and customarily exhibit toward one. The influence of these expectations can be deep and pervasive and can significantly influence performance. These unwritten rules or norms constitute a shadow organization which defines what is acceptable and often prescribes appropriate behavior.

Fritz Steele in *Consulting for Organizational Change*[3] suggests that norms or expectations exist at several levels: functional, operational, symbolic, and magical. Confusion results whenever one moves from a functional basis to a magical one for evaluating the performance of people at work. Consider for example, the differences in this illustration:

Maxim	Level
"You should work hard and be committed in order to be well regarded in this organization."	Functional
"You should come in early and stay late when needed in order to be well-regarded in this organization."	Operational
"You should work at least 60 hours a week in order to be well-regarded in this organization."	Symbolic
"You should arrive by 6:30 a.m. and not leave before 6:00 p.m. in order to be well-regarded in this organization."	Magical

Norms can be assets or liabilities depending on their focus, content, and intensity. They can contribute to productivity or limit it. Actually, norms are the unwritten rules and policies which operate in an organization. They are the "way things are done around here" and include procedures that everyone abides by despite their not being included in the policy manuals. These unwritten rules, while usually not discussed openly, tend to have as much effect as anything else on individual output and organizational effectiveness.

On pages 132 and 133 is an exercise in identifying and describing norms that exist in your working unit and in the division or department in which you work. Evaluating norms can be the basis for deciding whether they currently are functional or not. The primary purpose of this exercise is to *describe* what happens and not to *prescribe* what should be happening.

Perhaps understanding the norms that operate in the organizations of which we are a part is as important as any work activity we can undertake. Sometimes norms can be changed, especially when they are dysfunctional, by showing their disruptive and nonproductive effects. Importantly, they can be used, if properly understood, to encourage striving and achievement in any organization. Subordinates too can do much to

	Applies generally; usually helpful	Applies somewhat; usually helpful	Doesn't apply	Applies somewhat; usually harmful	Applies generally; usually harmful
1. There is a technical caste system in the company which values the contribution of highly mobile technical people more than that of nontechnical people.					
2. Never write to or show up at a manager's office without a recommendation of some kind for action on his or her part.					
3. Be cautious in asserting "facts." Almost always, someone in a meeting will hold a different point of view.					
4. The higher up in the organization a person is, the more he or she is permitted to hedge.					
5. The problems and opportunities which can be supported quantitatively will be the ones which will receive the most attention.					
6. In formal communications, managers communicate with managers rather than with the people working the problem.					
7. Upward feedback (information flowing "up" the hierarchy rather than "down" it) tends to be discounted or considered as comparatively unimportant.					
8. External problems and pressures must be given priority over internal repercussions and concerns.					
9. Unless people like you, they will tend to have less confidence in your analyses of problems and recommended solutions.					
10. A good salesperson does not miss a chance to make a sale even if a customer doesn't need the product.					

	Applies generally; usually helpful	Applies somewhat; usually helpful	Doesn't apply	Applies somewhat; usually harmful	Applies generally; usually harmful
11. No one openly criticizes a proposal made by a superior. Disagreements are voiced in private discussions.					
12. Regardless of whether or not someone feels angry or frustrated, such feelings must not be expressed on the job.					
13. People are reluctant to try new ideas or take risks because of the negative consequences which result if things don't work out just right.					
14. It is all right to say "I don't know, I'll find out" but not more than one-quarter of the time.					
15. Individual achievement is more important than the success of the work unit.					
16. Money for capital investment is easier to obtain than money for personnel development.					
17. To be accepted in this unit, you must be properly initiated and pay the appropriate dues (i.e., tell ethnic jokes, drink Lone Star Beer, attend church, dress well, etc.).					
18. Work comes before anything else.					
19. No one reads memos. To convey information you must pick up the phone or call a meeting.					
20. Loyalty to the boss is an expected quality for every employee to possess.					

create positive work norms, and they must not seem reliant upon the boss for direction.

Many organizations in recent years have attempted to increase the output of individual members through planned-change efforts. Such organization development attempts in what has been labeled the "social system" (the relationships between people on the job) have subsequently been categorized as team building. By and large, team-building designs implicitly or explicitly emphasize the value of collaboration and operate from the assumption that increased interaction and mutual discussion will improve existing conditions. One observer, in fact, maintains that the participation model is the only one which has been developed in the entire field of organization development.[4]

Many managers wonder if there is not some other way to resolve residual issues in the social system besides getting together to talk about them. What in particular can be done about a situation where people seem to know and understand what they should do, but still fail to do it? What options are available?

A significant accumulation of data suggests that a different kind of approach to planned-change efforts may hold a great deal of promise. Two management professors, Gene Dalton[5] and Abraham Korman,[6] argue that organization development's key objective should be to raise self-confidence and self-esteem. Consequently, efforts which in some way alter a person's self-image may provide a means to initiate and sustain planned-change efforts.

Self-esteem is a frequently discussed issue in both the popular literature and professional journals. Popular writers such as Clement Stone, Maxwell Maltz, Dale Carnegie, and Norman Vincent Peale, along with such academicians as Abraham Maslow, Rensis Likert, and B. F. Skinner, have all emphasized the importance of self-esteem. They differ in how they measure it and what they think affects it, but they are in agreement that its effects are significant. From all the available literature on self-esteem, two things seem to stand out more than any others in indicating how an adult derives a subjective self-evaluation, that is, develops self-esteem.

First, it appears that an adult's self-esteem is largely socially influenced. That is, people tend to perceive and define themselves according to how they believe other people perceive and define them. This proposition has a cadre of proponents.[7]

A second dimension which significantly influences self-esteem is the combined interplay of a person's level of aspiration and sense of achievement. Too few successes or too little aspiration results in a poor self-evaluation.[8] It is the degree to which successes approach expectations in those areas that are important to people that becomes their measure of achievement and, in turn, of themselves.

This explanation of the role of self-esteem and the forces which influence it leads to some important propositions regarding planned-change efforts. One such proposition is that effective planned-change efforts should capitalize on the influence of "significant others." The empirical support for this proposition is impressive. It has been found, for instance, that people often will believe or do what a prestigious source suggests; that patients who merely have contact with a prestigious medical authority improve significantly over waiting list controls (the "hello–good-bye" effect seen earlier); that subjects in an experiment will often do what an experimenter wants them to do, even though the experimenter is not consciously trying to influence them; and that setting goals for a person in the name of such authorities as "science" or "research" improves performance.[9] The common factor in all these studies seems to be that goals are being set for people by sources they respect.

Another proposition regarding planned change is that such efforts should alter the aspiration level and provide a sense of accomplishment to participants. The research efforts conducted by David McClelland, a Harvard professor, and John Miner, a management consultant, describe the impact of this effect. If one cognitive construct is substituted for another, a person's ability to perform is enhanced. What this means is that a person's self-image changes and her or his ability to perform is thereby increased.

The explanation lies in part in its symbolic nature. Learned acts have limited influence because they depend on reality supports (as in typewriting), but learned thoughts (symbolic acts) can occur anytime, anyplace, anywhere, and be applied to any situation.

The implication for planned change is the recognition that thoughts, once acquired, gain more control over thoughts and actions than acquired acts do, because they are harder to inhibit. Thoughts are symbolic acts, and when a person is given the opportunity to practice such symbolic acts, the tendency to transfer such symbolism to real situations is enhanced.[10] This means that in order to facilitate a change in the way a group of individuals perform a specific task, one must give them more than practice sessions in the performance of such a task. They must also do more than talk things out concerning the way things have been done in the past and the advantages of doing them differently in the future. They must instead come to think of themselves differently and be able to tie thought to action.

All of this indicates a direction which perhaps holds promise for those who engage in planned-change efforts. These implications seem to be particularly appropriate for a situation in which people already know what they should do but for some reason, are not performing as they indicate they should. When, after thoroughly gathering data, a planned-change facilitator discovers that the cause of a group's dysfunctional interaction is neither a lack of information nor an internal conflict, but instead a performance deficiency in an area of acknowledged proficiency, an intervention incorporating the previously discussed dimensions may be appropriate.

Since employees' on-the-job behavior is a function of both their own expectations of what they think they should do and the expectations which others hold and customarily exhibit toward them, an effective planned-change effort must somehow incorporate both. The influence of the expectations of others can be especially deep and pervasive and is the essence of the "Pygmalion effect." These combined influences concerning how a person should perform constitute a set of role expectations. Persons are essentially left on their own to notice individually *how* they should each perform their various tasks and fulfill their various assigned responsibilities. Sometimes people get conflicting messages regarding how they should perform, and they contradict the unwritten rules regarding the "way things are done around here." The consequences can be severe or mild, but are invariably disruptive.

Goal Setting and Participation

The English philosopher Jeremy Bentham once wrote that "Nature has placed mankind under the governance of two sovereign masters: pain and pleasure." His observation seems to fit as well today as when it was first written in 1822, because of the various anxieties as well as possible rewards faced by people. Organizational life, in particular, carries with it both pains and pleasures. Anxiety over doing well, disappointment when passed over for a promotion, fear of failure when making an oral report are simply examples of the types of anxieties and pains faced by people in organizations. Among the pleasures are feelings of achievement, competence, power, recognition, and affiliation. In short, feeling good about one's self and being well thought of.

The intensity which these several pleasures and pains are felt varies, but they do seem to govern our actions as human beings. There is a notion in current psychological research called "expectancy theory" which explains how pleasure and pain affect people and predispose them to take a particular course of action.[11] The central idea of expectancy theory is that people behave as they do because they believe that pursuing a particular course of action will lead to a pleasure (or reward) they value, or will avoid a pain (or anxiety). Expectancy theory stresses that people must believe or expect two things: first, that if they try to do something, they will succeed at it, that is, that they have ability to perform; and second, that their efforts and striving will be rewarded.

All of this is important background information because the central notion of the last 20 years or so in the field of organization development is that participation produces effort and striving and that externally imposed goals are anathema to this participation process. Jointly determined goals, it is held, will lead to better results. Douglas McGregor in his well-known book, *The Human Side of Enterprise*, described it this way:

> Genuine commitment is seldom achieved when objectives are externally imposed. Passive acceptance is the most that can be expected; indifference or resistance is the more likely consequence. Some degree of mutual involvement is necessary.[12]

But what is the evidence to support either approach—that imposing specific goals produces better results or that joint goal setting produces better results? Is one approach more likely to arouse anxiety and the other intrinsically more rewarding and pleasurable? What is the evidence for either approach?

Edwin Locke, a university researcher, has done more than perhaps anyone else to examine this question. Locke has found in a series of experiments that people produced more and did better on assigned tasks when they had specific goals rather than when they were simply urged to do their best.[13] It did not seem to matter whether they set the goals themselves or the goals were set by someone else. What did matter was that the goals were clear-cut and measurable—a point which sales and production managers intuitively recognize and use.

Goals are important. They specify intentions and establish standards. They direct the eye and focus attention. It appears that participation is not the key factor in goal setting; instead, having specific goals is. Most people crave certainty and predictability. We don't like to be surprised. We want to know where we are going and how we will be evaluated on our work performance. Having specific goals creates such order and instills certainty. It not only paves the way for achievement and recognition, but also reduces the uncertainty and anxiety concerning how one is likely to be judged by superiors at work, because the standards are known to all.

Setting challenging goals and requiring personal responsibility for results can also do much to arouse the latent need for achievement that is inherent in each person. Two basic aspects of achievement-stimulating goals have been identified through research:

- Achievement motivation will tend to be aroused if goals are explicit since such specificity makes it easier for people to adopt them as their own internal standards of excellence.
- Achievement motivation will tend to be aroused if goals represent a moderate degree of risk.[14]

The research findings of G. H. Hofstede on the motivational effects of budgeting also provide support for these ideas. His work indicates that when a realistic and challenging budget is prepared and presented to operating groups, they are individually and internally stimulated to meet budget standards.[15] The mere fact of explicitly identifying what is expected stimulates effort and striving to perform what is expected.

How to Set Challenging Goals

A recent report from General Electric concluded that employees tend to be more satisfied with their jobs as more difficult goals are set in their work area, provided the goals are not unrealistic or seen as arbitrary. Effective goals conform to the following guidelines:

A goal must be:

1. *Conceivable.* You must be able to picture yourself having already accomplished the goal and then be able to identify clearly what the first step would be that you must take.
2. *Believable.* You must believe that you can achieve the goal. Has someone you have known accomplished this goal? Are you able to use that person as an example or role model of the things you must do to reach the goal?
3. *Controllable.* If your goal includes the involvement of someone else, you should get that person's agreement to participate or to share resources.
4. *Measurable.* Your goal must be stated so that it is measurable in time and quantity. You must have some way of knowing when you have reached your goal.
5. *Desirable.* Your goal should be something you want to do. It is true that you can do almost anything you want, but you cannot do everything you want. You must choose. Your goals must be capable of moving you to action.

One executive put these guidelines into practice by distributing them to the employees he supervised and asking them individually to set goals, outline what they needed from him to accomplish their goals, and be prepared to discuss their plans within 10 days. Then he called a meeting at which all employees were present and had them describe individually what they were going to do and what they needed from the boss. Not only did the employees accomplish all their goals, but more challenging goals were set each time this process was repeated. The executive found that peer pressure could be used to provide a better control mechanism for goal attainment than his own admonitions could.

Another variation of this technique was used by an oil company executive. He called members of his work group together and indicated that he wanted to improve the overall output of the unit. He then passed out the guidelines for goal setting, asked members to come up with some goals they were committed to and to give him a copy of them, and left the room. Without the boss's influence, the group came up with some creative goals which they all agreed to and all worked on until each goal was realized.

Sometimes the success of such goal setting is thought to be due to employee participation. Although such involvement is very useful in many cases, the real key to success is the fact that goals are specific and explicit. The specificity of the goals enables each employee to use them as criteria in setting priorities for her or his own work. Not having specific goals in an organizational unit is like having a race in which the finish line is unannounced and unmarked. Consequently, the participants don't know whether to jog or sprint.

Setting explicit performance goals improves motivation because it makes accomplishments that are often overlooked explicit. One of the purest acts of leadership is this process of setting goals and getting others to work toward them. It is a key to both motivation and productivity. Moreover, allowing employee discretion in achieving objectives is also vital.

Too often, executives tend to govern activity instead of controlling direction. They get caught up in what George Odiorne, dean of the School of Business at the University of Massachusetts, calls the "activity trap." Odiorne says that in an activity-oriented organization it is possible to improve competence without improving output. This is because people are getting better and better at activities which do not count. Moreover, this activity orientation stifles motivation because there is no room for individual creativity or innovation.

In 1965 *Time* magazine asked the Ford Motors whiz kid Lee Iacocca the secret of his very successful managerial style. "How do I manage?" replied Iacocca. "At the beginning of every quarter, I sit down with every manager who works for me, and we talk about 'what are you going to produce for me during the coming year.' That's his commitment."

Iacocca went on to emphasize that he then acts as a resource to each manager, but he doesn't meddle in the manager's methods. He sets the pace and keeps the focus on direction and lets each manager be creative in his or her approach.

After being convinced that an assignment has been appropriately explained and fully understood, a manager should let employees use their own methods for achieving the project's desired outcomes. Creativity suffers under close, controlling supervision. President Theodore Roosevelt said it this way: "The best executive is the one who has sense enough to pick good men to do what he wants done, and self-restraint enough to keep from meddling with them while they do it."

A system of managing, then, that is centered on getting everyone committed to goals and allowing discretion in achieving them is both functional and developmental. It makes money while at the same time fostering a climate that permits people to grow. It is effective because it builds on people's natural desire for achievement and success.

There are many signs which indicate that carrot-and-stick techniques governing activity are ineffective. They may get movement, but they do not get motivation. In order to get others to be motivated, a manager must provide opportunities for people to succeed on the job and let success act as an incentive for improvement. It can be powerful, and it is probably the only way to get lasting commitment from employees and not merely short-term compliance.

Change is an integral part of every supervisor's, every manager's, every executives's job regardless of the types of organizations they are members of. Moreover, helping people improve and perform better is just as vital as changing organizational structures or creating technological breakthroughs. Four factors have been outlined in this chapter as principles which help another person change: manifesting personal concern, structuring positive payoff, helping reframe a situation, and setting explicit goals. Each of these factors works because it enhances self-esteem by helping a person deal more positively with his or her personal world as well as organizational life.

But let's be clear about one point: change seldom proceeds from one clear-cut, discrete, logical step to another. Sometimes it occurs in inexplicable spurts, while at other times it seems to be agonizingly slow. In helping others change, it is not necessary to understand complex theories of how individual personalities develop or operate. People are complex and different, it is true, but they are also very similar in some fundamental ways. These similarities and how they affect the ways people change need to be understood; extraneous bits of wisdom on personality development are of little help. It is the similarities in people and the processes concerning how they change that make the difference.

Summary

People change for many different reasons. Self-esteem is based on a variety of experiences. However, despite these facts, there is a consistent *process* of personal and interpersonal change that both affects and builds upon people's sense of self-esteem. Self-esteem is not a commodity, it is true. It is not something that a person either does or does not have. It is instead a consistent evaluation which we make of ourselves that includes an assessment of our abilities, limitations, and capabilities. It is a customary evaluation which we make which changes and can be changed. However, since it is so powerfully affected by our past experiences, our aspirations, our circle of friends and associates whose opinions we value, and our own workday activities, altering one's self-assessment is difficult. After all, how can a few new experiences compete with a lifetime of evaluations of prior experiences? The only easily made changes are cosmetic ones, and even they seem to get more difficult as people get older.

This chapter has suggested that a variety of current organizational problems—and their potential solutions—lie in better understanding the causes, correlates, and consequences of individual self-esteem. By explicitly analyzing the nature and dimensions of individual self-esteem, it becomes apparent that we maintain this self-evaluation with the active support and contribution of the groups we are a part of—whether we like it or not. We do not exist in a vacuum, and the people who are a part of our everyday lives influence us in indirect ways that often go unnoticed. In fact, the norms that govern the groups we are a part of may govern our actions more than formal policies or rules do. These silent, unspoken characteristics define what is right and proper and establish the yardsticks by which we instinctively judge our own efforts. Understanding how these processes work is the beginning of consciously managing them so as to improve our own lives and personal competency, as well as the lives and competency of others. Increasing our competency and our ability to give ourselves praise in evaluating our work is what building self-esteem is all about.

References

1. Zand, Dale: "The Impact of an Organization Development Program on Perceptions of Interpersonal, Group, and Organizational Functioning," *Journal of Applied Behavioral Science*, 5:393–410 (1969).
2. Zimbardo, Phillip: *Shyness* (Reading, Mass.: Addison-Wesley, 1977).
3. Steele, Fritz: *Consulting for Organizational Change* (Amherst: University of Massachusetts Press, 1981).

4. Strauss, George: *Organization Development: A Reappraisal* (Berkeley: University of California Press, Berkeley, 1979).
5. Dalton, Gene W.: "Influence and Organizational Change," in J. B. Ritchie and P. H. Thompson (eds.), *Organization and People* (St. Paul, Minn.: West, 1980).
6. Korman, Abraham: *Industrial and Organization Psychology* (Englewood Cliffs, N.J.: Prentice-Hall, 1971).
7. Hill, Norman C., and J. B. Ritchie: "The Effect of Self-Esteem on Leadership and Achievement: A Paradigm and a Review," *Group and Organization Studies* (December 1977).
8. King, Albert S.: "Expectation Effects in Organizational Change," *Administrative Science Quarterly*, 19:221–230 (1974).
9. Stogdill, Ralph J.: *Handbook of Leadership* (New York: Free Press, 1974).
10. Royce, James: *Psychology and the Symbol* (New York: Random House, 1965).
11. Porter, Lyman W., and Edward E. Lawler: *Managerial Attitudes and Performance* (Homewood, Ill.: Irwin-Dorsey, 1968).
12. McGregor, Douglas: *The Human Side of Enterprise* (New York: McGraw-Hill, 1960).
13. Locke, Edwin A.: "Toward a Theory of Task Motivation and Incentives," *Organizational Behavior and Human Performance*, 3:157–189 (1968).
14. Litwin, George H., and Robert A. Stringer: *Motivation and Organizational Climate* (Boston: Division of Research, Harvard Business School, 1968).
15. Cited in Joseph W. Atkinson, *Motivation and Achievement* (New York: Winston, 1974).
16. Odiorne, George: *Management Decisions by Objectives* (Englewood Cliffs, N.J.: Prentice-Hall, 1982).

Chapter 10

Managerial Actions and Organizational Improvement

We all have an image of who we are, a sense of self that suggests what is appropriate. We also have an idealized sense of self (a dream) about what is possible for us. In our early twenties, we are compelled by our desire to obtain our dream, to realize whatever goals we have set for ourselves. But somehow, somewhere along the way through life, many people lose their dreams and with it lose all sense of striving. They become, instead, content with things as they are. Striving becomes too much trouble, and change not worth the effort. Contentment, complacency, apathy creep into individual lives and become the dominant personal norm. Yet, people can and do change when provided the right incentive and motivation. Some alcoholics go dry; some heart attack victims change their lifestyles; some smokers decide to quit and, then, do, and some people go on diets and lose weight. What differentiates those who successfully make these personal changes and those who try and fail?

There are, of course, different reasons for different people. We are not exactly alike in our personality makeup or in our physical attributes. But although what we strive for may vary, as well as our relative success in doing what we set out to do, we all strive and we all have goals we want to accomplish. We also have the potential to do more than we are doing regardless of our current level of achievement.

Is this just another cheer for a variation of the pop psychology theme of "you can do anything you want to do"? No and yes. No, because we are limited by our ability and our opportunity. We do not start life out equal, and in our race for our goals, whatever they may be, some have advantages that are difficult to overcome. Success in achieving our goals depends as much on the *goals* we set for ourselves as it does on our willingness to sacrifice to achieve those goals. Despite the fact that we may not all be able to *become* exactly what we want to become, we can at least get *better* at whatever we do and whatever we strive for. Too often we set only *destination* goals—we think about where we want to end up—and consequently may set ourselves up for frustration and disappointment if we don't get what we go after. We ignore, unfortunately, the fun of the journey—the *process* of becoming the type of person we want to become. It may not be possible for each of us to become president of our organization, business, or country, but we can develop presidential qualities.

The attempt to realize the potentialities of everyone may seem visionary and extravagant, yet it is eminently practical when judged by the criterion of organizational efficiency. The efficiency of an organization, if properly gauged, is measured by its appropriate use of human as well as financial resources. Many decisions that are considered matters of administrative detail to an organization, moreover, may concern just those factors that acutely affect the everyday lives of rank-and-file employees.

It is important to be responsive to people and their individual and collective need to feel competent and capable if those who run organizations are going to get their employees' best efforts. Productivity lags when people are unmotivated and uncommitted. Yet, commitment and motivation are factors to be developed, not simply demanded. They are developed—collectively and individually—by building the self-esteem of those in the organization.

Self-esteem, as has been demonstrated in earlier chapters, is the basis for individual productive functioning. It is not static, but a dynamic view of one's self that may change from situation to situation. For instance, I may see myself as capable and effective at work, but less sure and certain of myself at home. Confidence in one area does not necessarily spill over into another area.

Positive Thinking and Self-Esteem

It is not possible for people to help themselves or others gain more self-confidence merely through words or intellectual knowledge. A manager telling a subordinate "You lack self-confidence" may be telling the person something that he or she is already painfully aware of, but doesn't know how to correct. "Be more confident" is not very helpful.

It is not possible to help others gain self-confidence by reassuring them that they are valuable and worthwhile employees. People already low in self-esteem are often "star-struck." They have difficulty accepting praise or compliments because they see their own inadequacy with clarity and believe that others who do not also recognize it are being insincere and gratuitous ("You're just saying that to make me feel good").

Despite these observations, how we *think* about ourselves is important. And positive thinking can have a potent effect on our view of our abilities and capabilities, but only when it is *consistent* with our basic sense of self-worth. Positive thinking is reinforcing to those who *already* view themselves as capable of attaining their goals. However, it cannot help a person *develop* such a vision unless the person comes to regard himself or herself differently. Someone must have a different set of experiences or be forced to re-evaluate and reinterpret past experiences before positive thinking will be helpful. For better or for worse, self-esteem is developed and enhanced primarily through positive experiences. Memories of past success act to provide the self-confidence needed for present tasks and the impetus to tackle more challenging goals in the future. The folk wisdom of "Nothing succeeds like success" certainly seems to be true.

It is widely believed that most people never reach their full potential. People could do more if they really wanted to or were appropriately challenged. In fact, we see people who have less ability than others achieve difficult goals, while their counterparts seem equally committed to the realization of these same goals but fall short in their attainment. Why do some managers seem to be able to bring out the best in their subordinates while others obtain something less? Why do some staff people seem so eager to do all that is necessary to complete required tasks while the performance of others is sluggish? What are some of the factors which affect the pursuit of goals, which influence the quality of persistence of performance?

Negative Self-Esteem

Just as there are principles for the development of self-esteem, so too there are factors which diminish it. People who have a sense of little self-worth can generally be described as those who lack poise, cannot cope with ambiguity, despair when they cannot readily find solutions to their problems, and believe that most of their efforts are likely to fail. Their expectations of their ability and performance are low because they believe that they can do few things well. Although most people, from time to time, question their worth and their place in the organization that employs them, persons with little self-esteem maintain a constant and continuing image of themselves as "not fitting in." Because they feel awkward, they act awkwardly in social situations, a fact that helps to maintain a self-reinforcing cycle of expectation leading to behavior confirmed by experience.

It is important to realize that feelings of inadequacy stimulate some people to work harder to overcome their deficiencies. In fact, a frequent tool of organizational change is to survey employee opinions and to compare these with what top managers believe are desirable and attainable. This "disparity method" rests on the assumption that managers and others will want to close the gap between what "is" and what they think "ought to be." This method is also frequently used as an anonymous means of providing feedback to an individual manager by polling employees on how the manager actually manages and how they think the person ought to manage. However, for the person who already feels inadequate, such feedback may prove devastating. Perhaps the critical factor which distinguishes people who are truly high in self-esteem is their ability to accept their own weaknesses and not be threatened by the criticism of others. I have seen many otherwise capable persons who were ineffective as managers because they had not developed this characteristic. They bristled at criticism and blamed it on malcontents and complainers.

Under some circumstances, there is relatively little a manager can do to enhance the self-esteem of an employee because no amount of discussion, goal setting, and recognition can convince such persons that they can achieve. Their logic allows them to find proof for their assumption of failure, and objective reality is no match for what they believe themselves to be. They have a conviction, and they find the necessary experiences to support their conviction. Moreover, since perception is selective, they tend to perceive only those things which support their belief and ignore those which do not confirm their assumption.

The process of enhancing self-esteem is based on changes to be made in our beliefs, feelings, and expectations. To some extent, expectations are the most important since most of us tend to move in the direction of what we expect to occur. Changing our expectations, therefore, is pivotal to changing our behavior. It is at this point that past experiences become so important because they define current beliefs, predispositions, and expectations. Experiences that have resulted in prior failures color one's willingness to try again and lead a person to expect to fail.

Organizational Systems

A massive study was undertaken a few years ago at General Electric to determine the effectiveness of the company's performance appraisal system. The results were surprising and disconcerting. The investigators found that their appraisal system actually resulted in a deflating experience and accounted for decreased performance because overall it had a negative effect on employees' self-esteem. GE researchers found that the evaluation system used in the company, which forced supervisors to slot performers into a percentage distribution approximating a normal distribution or bell-shaped curve and to inform them of their relative position, had several unintended negative consequences: disruptive competition, decreased motivation, and lowered overall morale.[1]

Perhaps the strongest effect of such a system is the impact it has on a manager's *thinking*. A manager who knows it is necessary to tell subordinates where they fit on a well-defined performance hierarchy is almost forced to begin thinking of them and regarding them as either above average or at the bottom of the heap. Once this view of employees is established, they will sense it and be affected by the manager's expectations. As one engineer who works under such a system has said:

> If your supervisor comes to believe that you are worthless, and he begins to treat you that way, it's very hard to fight. You can tell yourself you're still a good engineer, but you've got to have a very strong ego. If he continues to lower your rating in future years, it gets to you.

There is, of course, a need to evaluate people in a large organization in order to distribute rewards and select future managers. Unfortunately, these purposes are not well served in many companies. People who run organizations have a need for information and a need to determine the direction of the enterprise. These ends will not be achieved as well as they might be if they diminish the self-esteem of the organization's employees, however.

Control systems, like evaluation systems, can diminish self-esteem if not properly structured. People have a need to feel that they exercise some personal control over their workaday lives and a need to be informed of organizational matters that will affect them. Powerlessness and arbitrary decisions not only make employees angry but can directly affect their output and performance. People want to feel in control of their world and matters which affect them directly.

A paternalistic pact is sometimes made between employees in an organization and top managers. It is not unique to workers on the shop floor, and in fact is more characteristic of professional employees. This pact is one in which employees implicitly say, "You know what's best for me. If I work hard, you'll watch out for my interests," and top managers implicitly respond, "Don't worry, I know what's good for you, and I'll take care of you." Such pacts give rise to paternalistic practices which themselves are self-fulfilling prophecies: people are dependent on the support of top managers, and top managers interpret such dependence as a request for more control. This is not to say that all external control and dependence is bad, but certainly giving enough information and authority to employees so that they can exert a significant amount of self-control and independence is good. Decentralization, which allows decisions to be made at the lowest possible level where there is accurate information, is an ideal which many organizations espouse but which too few practice.

Self-Esteem and Social Support

We enhance our self-esteem through our relationships with other people. This is important to recognize. Our self-esteem is not something which is fixed, which remains constant through our lifetime, but rather is something which changes and is changeable. We periodically test our evaluation of ourselves with people who are important to us, and we are, consequently, recharged or deflated by our perceptions of what they think. This testing occurs especially when we undergo changes. A new job, a new work assignment, a new neighborhood are all occasions when we tend to re-evaluate who we think we are.

Each of these situations presents an opportunity for managers to actively build the confidence and esteem of those they supervise. Each "decision point" in the life of an employee is a chance for a manager to enhance that person's motivation and commitment. Research has shown that people attempt to behave in a fashion consistent with their own self-image. For instance, if employees in a particular work unit see themselves as failures on the job, they will not put forth much effort and their resulting performance will probably be poor. Such action will then reinforce the negative self-image. Thus, a clear-cut and practical managerial strategy to improve performance is to modify employees' self-image and enhance their self-esteem.

Decision points in people's lives are the times when they are most open to the influence of others. It is during these times that a person's self-image can be changed and self-esteem developed. Moreover, as long as people work together in an organization, it will not be possible for them to ignore the effects of their actions on each other. The real question, especially for managers, is not *will* they influence the self-esteem of employees, but *in what ways* will they affect employees' self-esteem. It is important to realize as well that what really counts is not what a manager says or intends but what an employee "hears." Probably few managers consciously want to tear down an employee's self-esteem, but their actions may nevertheless achieve that result. Because of their lack of self-awareness and social skills, they produce unintended and unwanted effects among employees.

Understanding yourself, building your confidence, and reaching to achieve your potential are all consistent themes in this book. Helping others get these same results is also an integral part of it. In fact, it is generally easier to do these three things for someone else than it is to do them for yourself. This is because all three are developed through supportive interaction with important others. People, truly, are social beings.

A physician is often in the position of having to reassure patients whose limbs have recovered from an accident or disease that their limbs "work okay." A manager must often do the same with respect to the self-image of employees. Sometimes this can be done by pointing out to people that their expectations for themselves are too high, or that they judge themselves too harshly or too unfairly, that they depreciate their achievements and depreciate their assets. A manager may need to reassure employees that they are indeed doing well. This in turn will give them some relief from self-demands and provide added strength toward mastering their problems.

One way to enhance the self-esteem of others is to be a mentor to certain employees in specific ways. The idea of a mentor reaches back into the Middle Ages where young men who wanted to learn a trade or artistic skill would apprentice themselves to recognized masters. The apprentice would agree to work hard and study often to learn the particular craft, and the mentor, in exchange, would agree to show the apprentice how to ply the trade.

The fact that almost everyone who joins a new organization from a college or professional school needs a mentor is widely recognized. Gene Dalton and Paul Thompson, two researchers associated with the department of organizational behavior at Brigham Young University, have found through interviewing almost 1000 engineering, accounting, and M.B.A. professionals in the past 10 years that those who are the most effective have found themselves a mentor to help them get off to a good start in their careers. What does this mentor do for the apprentice? Here is one description:

> He takes the younger man under his wing, invites him into the new occupational world, shows him around, imparts his wisdom, cares, sponsors, criticizes, and bestows his blessing.

Developing the self-esteem of others and creating high performance expectations that become self-fulfilling prophecies are a natural result of a mentor-apprentice relationship. The attention, support, direction, and challenge that a mentor provides are some of the basic ingredients necessary in the successful use of the Pygmalion effect as a managerial tool.

We often overlook just how much support we all need. Our ability, however, to face conflicts and resolve problems depends on the support we get from others. People working in the same organization can develop close working relationships that help them achieve some desired standard together, or they can remain a group of strangers who simply share some common space for a certain period of the day. But since we all need support to face the conflicts and anxieties that are a part of living, the more sources for support we have, the better we are able to cope.

The widespread growth in recent years of such support groups as Weight Watchers, Alcoholics Anonymous, and encounter groups illustrates the search many people are engaged in for support. Each of us needs and wants acceptance. Meeting regularly with a group of people who have common purposes is one way to partially satisfy this very human need. It provides an opportunity to share with people we trust and to get recharged and renewed.

The potential for creating at the workplace support groups that develop self-esteem within each member and reinforce high performance expectations is significant. This can be done by redirecting the focus of many commonly held meetings and by making supportive group dialogue a routine part of managerial operations. In fact, the entire technology of organization development has been developed to make cohesive groups, whose members are mutually supportive, out of work units in industry where more coordination and better results are desired.

There are some very distinct advantages that can be obtained by making support groups out of work units. Besides providing support in times of stress and crisis, they can be settings where people learn to be trusting and helpful to one another. Second, they can be good problem-finding and problem-solving tools for dealing with work-related problems. Third, they are good vehicles for implementing change. They gain commitment from their members so that decisions are likely to be carried out. Fourth, they can control and discipline individual members in ways that are difficult through more formal authority channels. And, fifth, as organizations get bigger, small groups seem to be a useful tool for reducing the negative effects of largeness. It is a useful process which can produce desirable organizational results.

References

1. Kay, Emmanuel, and Richard Hastman: *An Evaluation of Work Planning and Goal Setting Discussions* (Crotonville, N.Y.: Behavioral Research Services, General Electric Company, 1966).

Index

About the Author

NORMAN C. HILL is Exxon's Southeastern Division Personnel Resources Supervisor. He is the author of several highly regarded books on management and personnel relations, including *Counseling at the Workplace* and *Increasing Managerial Effectiveness*.